Twentieth-Century
French
Thought

Also by Joseph Chiari

The Aesthetics of Modernism
Anthology of French Poetry
Britain and France, the Unruly Twins
Columbus's Isle
Contemporary French Poetry
Corsica, the Scented Isle
The Eagle of Prometheus (*poems*)
T. S. Eliot, Poet and Dramatist
France and the War
France and the Problems of Peace
The French Contemporary Theatre
Impressions of People and Literature
Landmarks of Contemporary Drama
Lights in the Distance (*poems*)
Mary Stuart (*verse play*)
The Necessity of Being
Paradoxes (*poems*)
The Poetic Drama of Paul Claudel
Realism and Imagination
Reflections on the Theatre (*translation*)
Religion and Modern Society
Symbolisme—from Poe to Mallarmé
White Temple by the Sea (*poems*)

Twentieth-Century French Thought

From Bergson to Lévi-Strauss

Joseph Chiari

Docteur ès Lettres

GORDIAN PRESS
NEW YORK
1975

B
2421
.C48
1975

Printed in Great Britain

Contents

Preface

This book is a critical examination of twentieth-century French thought, from Bergson to structuralism, including phenomenalism, existentialism—atheistic and religious—and thinkers like Simone Weil, Teilhard de Chardin and Bachelard, and it is also a speculative exploration of the ideas, perennial or new, at work during that period.

The critical aspect of this study rests, above all, on analyses of the various philosophical systems examined and on comparisons and differences between them, rather than on searches for verbal or syntactic meanings. The speculative aspect aims at apprehending the main ideas that inform the society to which the philosophers concerned belong. The apprehension of these ideas is, up to a point, a matter of individual sensibility, imagination and affinities; their coordinated verbal characterisation should be a matter of reason.

The overall principle underlying this study could be said to flow from Heraclitus, *Fragment 50*, which reads as follows : 'If you have attended, not to myself as such, but to the meaning of what I have said, then it is wise to say that, according to this meaning, all things are one.' The philosopher, whether he searches for the truth of being, as far as mind and reason can reach, or for the truth of certain aspects of being at the individuated or social level, is always part of his time, is significant in as far as he expresses its living consciousness and sensibility, and achieves greatness in as far as he goes beyond it and expresses some more or less important aspects of the human psyche that transcend time and place. These rather summarily stated and, no doubt, arguable views are put forward only in order to act as guide lines for the understanding of the general

pattern and unfolding of this book. They should help the reader
to appreciate the reasons why some philosophers, like Lalande
or Jean Wahl, have not been discussed, and why others, like
Maritain, have not been given the space to which the bulk of
their philosophical work might have entitled them. A critique is
neither an apologia, nor a defence, nor an argument aiming at
a final conclusion; the reader is left with the opportunity of
drawing his own, and this is something that precludes any
artificial, neatly phrased summing up, or prophecies about
tomorrow.

Introduction

Ideas are the mental projections of the forces that underlie man's mental apprehension of the universe and shape the reality of history. The pattern of ideas, like the pattern of the various forces at work in history, is therefore constantly changing, passing from contrasts to identity, from identity to contrasts, like sand ceaselessly sieved by the sea. The changes on the plane of ideas are more a question of emphasis according to historical time than a question of absolute transformations and total disappearances. Ideas, in fact, never disappear completely; they follow the patterns of nature, and, like shells woven by years of silent life, their mysterious beauty emerges under a new shape and challenges the mind to probe depths which it cannot reach. The pattern of ideas could, like the pattern of biological evolution, be represented by a tree with its trunk or central idea—cause and subsistence of life—and various branches which, whatever the form of society to which they relate, connect through their essence with the central idea which informs and sustains life.

This view of life excludes any dualism between matter and mind, a notion no longer tenable in our times, when the equation between matter and energy and their interchangeability has been scientifically established. This does not mean, of course, that mind is coextensive with matter any more than the brain is coextensive with thought. There is a close relationship between the two, and the growth and evolution of life rests entirely upon the properties of the chemical elements which compose it, yet, although one may know what these chemical elements are, one does not know exactly why they possess certain appetitions or attributes which make them either join together or diverge, and

9

any laboratory analysis of their chemical components results merely in a tautological statement of what they are, not in the knowledge of why they are so. They are what they are, and we know what they are at the given moment at which we choose to analyse them, but we do not know exactly how and why they have reached the stage at which our analysis takes places, any more than we know or will ever know the true nature and reality of the infinite universe of which they are part.

Just as there is no possible separation between body and mind, there is no separation between nature and man. Man is an integral part of nature, and his mind, which enables him increasingly to understand nature, contains in itself ideas of the structures of the laws of nature. The actualisation of ideas corresponding to and representing forces at work in history makes them part of man's consciousness, and as such, they activate the movement and development towards greater and greater complexification and self-knowledge, which seems to be the true finality of organic life. Genius at the artistic, scientific or philosophical level reveals the true being of life and of its laws, and thus fosters the unfolding of this self-knowledge. Everything in life, whether on the mental plane or on the natural plane, appears as coherent and inextricably interconnected, so that all changes and fluctuations, either in the life of the earth or in the life of the mind, are causally related and parts of an unfolding pattern which leaves no room for chance or for absolute novelty or originality. Everything in the life of man, at the political, economic, artistic or mental level, takes place as a continuation of, or reaction to, what preceded, and re-emerges as fragments of previous syntheses of ideas which had gone underground, to reappear at the moment when they correspond to social realities. Ideas remain alive and active as long as the social forces which they correspond to are alive, that is to say, are active and calling for actualisation. These forces are opposed or counteracted by others with which they form partial syntheses, something that naturally entails partial rejections of what cannot be absorbed by society at a given moment, that is to say generally the most advanced aspects of the ideas at work in the society. These rejections form the basis of other forces which will replace the previous syntheses from which they had been excluded, and which will, in turn, break up into positive elements which will be socially active and into negative elements which will lie dormant until they can become part of new living forces; so that, in the end, the notion of positive and negative is continuously changing.

Human thought is like the sea. It has its heights and its troughs, its backwaters and its eddies, its calm moments and its moments of violence and turmoil; but, like the sea, it is one, and deep down it connects with the elemental forces which make life and movement possible. Human thought is not a pure abstraction, or some kind of kite floating above the everyday life of mankind. It is an integral part of it; it emanates from it, and it both reflects it and modifies it. The various oscillations of human thought are the oscillations of civilisations and of history, which both cause them and are affected by them.

The complexities and variations of Western thought can be traced back to their basic Hellenic-Judaic roots, some two thousand five hundred years ago. For Plato, the life of man was only a dream, a spume on the fringe of the ocean of Eternity, which the soul, laden with memories of the real world, had crossed so as to be imprisoned in a human body, but which it would soon re-cross, after the death of the body, to be cleansed and purified in order to return to the ideal world, the world of the blessed, something not unrelated to the Buddhist nirvana. Knowledge was memory, and as Plato put it in the *Timaeus*, 'God being unable to make the world eternal, gave it time as the moving image of Eternity.' History did not matter, for in a world in continuous flux, the attempt to fix and to record singular or significant instants was meaningless. Yet, as we know, in spite of these beliefs, Plato was anything but detached from the affairs of the world, and a good deal of his philosophic thinking, like that of his great master Socrates, is devoted to teaching men the best way to govern themselves according to the law, which is the law of God. Besides, one must not forget that Greek thought was not unified, and that while Platonic thought gave pre-eminence to the ideal world of God and the Essences, Protagoras asserted that man was the measure of all things.

The Judaic world stresses, on the other hand, the importance of existence and history. The Incarnation gives meaning to history, and the fact that immanence is continuously connected with transcendence means that God is always present in the life of His people. The Greek gods had their own business to attend to, and besides, they themselves were not entirely free from the iron rules of necessity. Neither the gods nor men could, in the end, transgress the Law with impunity, and though the gods' actions towards men or other demi-gods who challenged their power look at first sight arbitrary, they were, in the end, deeply rational and faithful to their belief in supreme justice and in an equilibrium which could not be disturbed with impunity. The main problem for man was to know the Law, and great thinkers like Plato and Socrates, law-givers like Solon, demi-gods like Prometheus or goddesses like Minerva endeavoured to reveal to men the Law that they had to obey and the justice they had to respect. To know the Law was to be conscious of one's own sources and one's own ties with the Divine. The soul was the mediating link between the world of Time and the Divine, or True Being. 'Know thyself', said Socrates, and to know oneself it is necessary to know one's true connection with, and dependence upon, true being. This notion that true knowledge is the knowledge of true being and the only basis of freedom does, in fact, span Western thought, from Plato and Socrates to Augustine, Kant, Hegel and Bergson, and is one of its most important aspects. The great difference between the 'know thyself' of the Greeks and the Christian knowledge of true being is that the Greek consciousness of Necessity, acquired through self-knowledge, entailed the inescapable acceptance of the laws of Necessity, while the Christian knowledge of true being which is love, entails a willing and loving cooperation between the Creator and creation, in order to realise His purpose which is absolute knowledge and absolute love.

The Greeks were not only concerned with knowing themselves, they were also concerned with knowing the perfect rationality of nature and of the universe, and in this latter case, to know meant to be able to control or to predict the various aspects of the life of the universe. This type of knowledge did not rest upon mystical revelations or memories of the soul's ethereal origins, but upon the observations and mathematical laws which are the basis of the scientific attitude, which is, in fact, as much a part of

Greek thought as Pythagorean or Platonic mysticism. Aristotle was its greatest representative, and with the exception of a brief interregnum of neo-Platonism which dominated the first centuries of Christianity, Christian thought became more and more conscious of the rationality of belief in the Divine, and of the importance of reason as a means of discovering and mastering the laws of nature. With Thomas Aquinas, the Platonic-Augustinian concept of knowledge through the mediation of the soul or of God is finally replaced by the concept of rationalistic realism. Platonic and Augustinian angelic flights transcending Time are replaced by the creativity of human consciousness working in continuous Time, God-orientated and carrying creation to Him. This change entailed another just as important, and which is the transition from the concept of life as a transient, shadowy passage on earth, during which the soul waits for its liberation from the body, to the concept of life on earth as of vital importance for the kind of fate that the soul or essence will have in after-life. Existence is informed with essence, not in the sense of being a kind of Platonic or Hindu appearance tied to the wheel of Time and waiting for liberation through death, but, on the contrary, as the image of the Incarnation, and therefore the means by which the Creator fulfils His creativity and makes it possible for the soul or essence to achieve or not achieve final union with true being. Thence of course the vital importance of life in time, and the urge constantly to improve life through knowledge and through mastery of the laws of nature.

Knowledge is power, and from Thomas Aquinas, Roger Bacon and Ockham until about the end of the nineteenth century, practically everything conformed to the laws of reason, and rationalism in its various forms dominated Western thought. 'If you look at the world rationally,' said Hegel, 'it looks back rationally at you.' Faith itself was, on the whole, rational, and all great thinkers from Aquinas to Pascal, Descartes, Locke, Spinoza and Leibniz found that faith was rational, or that, if it could not be rationally proved or disproved, it was rational, as Locke said, to assent to it, or as Pascal, very Lockian in many ways, put it, to leap into it. Up to Descartes, the world was one, and transcendence and immanence were continuously linked, through Grace and through the divine subsistence which

informed creation. Yet the Cartesian separation of body from
soul, matter from spirit, thought from its object, creation from
Creator, connected with Him only through acts of continuous
creation, progressively favoured the raising of the immanent
thinking *I* to the level of transcendence. The time was soon ripe
for the separation of immanence from transcendence, which was
more and more relegated to a status of abscondence, so that man,
although fully aware that religion is, like fire, something inherent
in human culture, did not have to repudiate God, but put Him
in abeyance.

Seventeenth-century French society was strongly hierarchised
and still theocentric. The King was king by divine right, and the
social order was blessed and approved by the Church which
showed no more tolerance towards the Protestants or the
Jansenists than it had shown towards the Cathars. This was an
anti-rational attitude which could not but lead to the discrediting
of the Church and organised religion. England, which had not
hesitated to submit the divine right of kings to the judgment of
the people, nevertheless continued to believe in the Divinity, or
rather in the sacredness of authority and in a strongly hierarchised
society in which the importance of the trading and financial class
was steadily growing. Empirical rationalism was the dominant
philosophy of the day, and Lockian understanding made possible
an attitude of political and religious tolerance which was the
admiration of Europe, while the widespread notion of assent to
religious belief kept religion free from the acrimonious, rationalistic critique to which it was submitted in Voltairian France.

In France the aristocracy and the *haute bourgeoisie*, which
intermarried with the same aristocracy and supported the King
with money and administrative personnel, could have no other
attitude than that of being in favour of the established order,
while the peasants, crushed by poverty, and the small artisans,
who were little better off, had no political power and no strong
urge or means to overthrow this order. Yet, a middle class was
steadily emerging from the *artisanat* and from the benefits of the
expanding trade of the Western nations with their colonial
possessions, and with this changing shape of society, the ideas
that had been dominant hitherto were also changing. God
Who, in Cartesian philosophy, had ceased being looked upon as

an ever-watchful Father making His presence felt through His unfailingly righteous Church, was increasingly looked upon as a Creator Whom human beings could approach directly, through their individual conscience and sensibility.

The importance of the role of reason was growing. The causes of this growth are difficult to assess. Can they be ascribed to or at least linked with the economic conditions that were producing a new society with a growing middle class more and more prosperous and materialistic, better educated, more anthropomorphic and individualistic, and aspiring to a more rational type of life? These are certainly historical facts; yet, one cannot make of them the causes of certain spiritual and mental attitudes. Causes and effects are, in this domain, inextricably interconnected, and the concept that seems to me the most rational is that which looks upon a development in society and the life of mankind as a process of becoming which is self-caused and carries its own finality, and upon art, philosophy and politico-economic changes as expressing the varying stages of the unfolding of this process.

The eighteenth century, the age of reason, is not, strictly speaking, irreligious. Voltaire's battle cry *Ecrasez l'infâme* did not apply to religion; it applied to its dogmatism, its intolerance, its bigotry, fanaticism and obscurantism, which an adult rationalism could no longer accept. Rationality implied tolerance, and beliefs which could not be dealt with by the understanding could be given assent by the mind and the heart. Theology was no longer necessary, and God, *le Dieu sensible au coeur*, could be felt directly through the heart, in the manner best exemplified by Rousseau in the *Profession de foi du vicaire savoyard*, which echoes Pascal's words : 'We know truth, not only through reason, but also through the heart. It is through the latter that we know the first principles, and it is on knowledge from the heart and from the instinct that reason must base its discoveries.'* (*Pensées*, ed. Chevalier, p. 202) The 'heart' of Pascal and Rousseau is, it seems to me, Bergson's intuition and also the romantic imagination which apprehends the wholeness and essence of things.

'Even mathematics, natural philosophy and natural religion are in some measure dependent on the science of Man'; thus

---

* All translations from the French are the author's own.

Hume, who heralds the emergence of the importance of anthropology. Eighteenth-century man is on the move, towards the post-Hegelian, Feuerbachian notion that faith, truth and God Himself start from man, who lives in a world in which transcendence is in abeyance and only immanence matters. Sensibility and individual conscience, receptivity, quietism, pietism and communion with Nature in the solitude of mountains or forests, these are the ways not only to spirituality and illumination, but also to illuminism, spiritualism and all sorts of pseudo-religions, from Rosicrucianism to positivism, and to Robespierre's worship of *l'Etre Suprême*. Reason and sentiments become completely separated, and each has its own well-defined task. The result is that sentiments, unsieved by reason, turn to sentimentality, while reason, without sentiments, is dehumanised and engenders its own type of fanaticism and intolerance. Anthropology and psychology begin to take root, and they flourish more and more throughout the nineteenth and twentieth centuries. Man endeavours to take full control of his life, and God is merely kept in the background as a kind of ultimate Kantian absolute, to Whom one may have recourse as the final answer to a principle of morality or a mystery which one cannot solve. Well before Marx's encouragements, eighteenth-century man believes in taking a hand in the making of history, and before Darwin and Lamarck, he confers upon the spiritless matter of Descartes certain inherent aptitudes, affinities and capacities which anticipate Darwin's and Spencer's evolutionary theories, as well as Lamarck's transformism.

Kant marks the zenith of rationalism, even though he maintains the gap between practical and pure reason, which is bridged by Hegel, who with his words: 'The rational is the real' closes the cycle of rationalism begun with the Greeks. It is also Hegel who gives its philosophical form and coherence to the idea of evolutionary creation which, whether on the materialistic or on the idealistic plane, was the dominant idea of the nineteenth century. Marxism is a kind of evolutionism, and Darwin, Spencer and, later on, Bergson and Teilhard de Chardin were all aware, each with his own bias, that the world is a vast process of becoming, both coherent and organic. Such a unified vision of the world embraces, with their respective stresses, Marxism and

Christianity, as well as the world of science. History is for Hegel
the actualisation of spirit; for Marx it is the outcome of economic
forces; but in both cases, history is the work of man. The
Hegelian hero, like Napoleon, incarnates the *Zeitgeist* which
hastens the spiritualisation of life. The Marxist hero, like Lenin
or Mao Tse Tung, understands and guides the will of the masses
towards their liberation and towards the accomplishment of their
destiny. The final outcome of both systems is, in spite of their
different premises and processes, to reach a form of perfection,
a kind of city of God, something which is also the aim of all
religions.

A great philosophical system, expressing a coherent view of the
life and laws of the universe, is both a crystallisation of the ideas
and main forces that shape and express its time, and also a
mental representation of the life of the universe which, in as far
as it is the work of true genius, has validity for all times, in the
sense that it connects with, and continues, completes or refutes
in part, other philosophical systems which have preceded it and
which form part of a whole which is the human mind. There is
no more discontinuity in thought than there can be discontinuity
in the life of mankind, or in that of any given society, which is
part of it. The component elements of the life of a given society
are in a constant state of change, yet they are always closely
interconnected, and it is these interconnections which run
through the life of any society throughout historical time, and
which underlie the unavoidable connections between one given
philosophical system and another. This is not a question of
influences, paternities or filiations, it is merely the realisation of
the fact that art and philosophy express the society and the time
to which they belong, and that every moment of the life of a
society is necessarily connected with the one which, if time is
looked upon diachronically, seems to precede it but which, if
time is looked upon, as it ought to be, synchronically, seems to
have been, in some ways, always part of it.

The social and economic problems that a society faces at any
given time always have very deep and complex roots, and the
solutions that are applied to them are never truly new, though
they are of course conditioned by the time when they are
applied. The same process applies to art and to philosophy.

Romanticism, for instance, was the natural continuation of the individualism, the enthusiasm and the mixture of rationalism and subjectivism that marked the end of the eighteenth century. Marxism followed Hegelianism or pure idealism—part of the age—and therefore could not ignore it; it could only react against it and make use of it to analyse and to attempt to modify the stark economic and social conditions of the time, which were in contrast with it. The Hegelian *Zeitgeist*, transforming the real into the absolute, becomes, with Marx, the economic conditions which animate and transform matter in such a way as to reach not the absolute, but a kind of angelic stage in which all men will be brothers, and in which work will be pure, ever enjoyable creativity. It is a Messianic vision, as beatific as the abstract absolute of Hegel or the Christian City of God.

Between Marx and Hegel there are of course many representatives of thought and sensibility who correspond to, and therefore make it possible to sketch a map of, the mental, social and economic conditions of the age. There is Feuerbach, who marks the transition between the *Deus absconditus* of Kant, the abstract God of Hegel, and the dead God of Nietzsche. Feuerbach describes the essence of religion as human essence. 'Christian religion,' he says, 'is the behaviour of man towards himself, or rather towards his essence, but he behaves towards his essence as if it were an alien essence. The divine essence is more exactly the essence of man freed from the individual, existential being, objectified, that is to say contemplated and adored as an essence distinct from man himself and endowed with its own existence.' Feuerbach, like Freud, sees God as an objectification of man's feelings, yet if essence can be separated from the existent and be apprehensible as essence, it is obvious that it cannot issue from man himself, for it is not possible for an existent to apprehend himself as pure essence, without necessarily bringing in either the Cartesian transcendence which follows the *cogito* or Husserlian intentionality. Essence, if posited, can only issue from Being, something which makes it possible for the existent to apprehend his essence as objectification of an aspect of being. Feuerbach has, in fact, transferred to human essence—source of religion—all the attributes of essence which are part of Hegelian philosophy. Still, he does confirm a kind of immanentism which was already in Hegel and which Marx in due time transferred to matter and history. Man gradually diminishes God's attributes and increases his own. The Protestant religion naturally encouraged this humanisation of God as well as the growth of religious anthropology and Christology, with Christ practically alone on the human stage, without a father or a mother, and with only human brotherhood.

With Feuerbach there are Fourier and Saint-Simon, forerunners of Marx, there is Auguste Comte and positivism, and there is, above all, a Western society more and more dominated by the middle class, materialistically minded, intoxicated by the dreams of science, aware that it is the real basis of political power, and not caring much about God or His Church, except as an apparent means of maintaining its own authority. The Western world no longer has a centre; religion is no longer a living force. It is, on the whole, merely an appearance or an adornment for a class of society which, for its credibility, like Hans Andersen's Emperor, needs clothes, and uses for such a purpose religion and morality. The proletariat, aware of its alienation from this society, can no longer give its support to a faith that ignores its most crying needs, and therefore increasingly understands that justice lies in its hands and in its courage to fight for its human rights.

Life as it was at the end of the nineteenth and the beginning of the twentieth centuries was totally irrational and inhuman, and rationalism was discredited. The despair of Nietzsche, the nihilism of Dostoyevsky, are the best mirrors of the state of mind of the age. Reality was, for anyone who thought and felt deeply, more and more unbearable, and whether in art or in thought, men were driven further and further to the awareness that the only reality which they could explore and reveal was that of the heart and the mind of man, adrift in an irrational, science-obsessed world. The transcendental subjectivism of the poetry of Mallarmé, the Hegelianism, the 'to be or not to be' of Valéry, the abstractions and subjectivism of Cubism, the introspections of Proust, Gide or Joyce, reflect the frame of mind and the artistic sensibility of a society that has reduced its values to success, well-being and material comfort, leaving little room for true art or Carlylean heroes or Nietzschean supermen.

In this society, psychology has been in the ascendancy since the second half of the nineteenth century, with Charcot and Janet practising the first deep explorations of the subconscious and the first treatment of mental disturbances by hypnosis and psychoanalytical methods, which Freud followed and applied. William James's studies of the stream of consciousness show the same preoccupations as Bergson's. Last, but not least, the Einsteinian relativistic notion of time marks a break from the Newtonian mechanistic notion of time, and parallels the Bergsonian notion of duration to which, as we shall see, it is not unrelated.

I

Henri Bergson

Henri Bergson (1859–1941) was part of the sensibility of his age, and he expresses certain important aspects of it. This sensibility was extremely fragmented, and his philosophy more or less encompasses it, in the same way as Kantianism encompasses eighteenth-century rationalism, or Hegelianism nineteenth-century idealism and romanticism. The France of Bergson is also the France of Comtian positivism, whose main tenet is that science is the only legitimate mode of knowledge. It is the France of Cubism and Symbolism which, in their various aspects, rest upon idealism and give to aesthetic knowledge a subjective basis and, in the case of poetry, a transcendental value. It is also the France of evolutionary biology, psychology, spiritualism, naturalism in the novel and in the theatre, positivistic materialism in sociologists like Durkheim, and social conflicts like the famous Dreyfus case.

Bergson is opposed to the type of limited rationalism, shorn of Humean subtleties or of Kantian distinguos, which is Comtian positivism. He has been accused of irrationalism, anti-intellectualism, and even of hollow though elegant verbalism. These seem to be the views of writers and critics who have their own axes to grind and who mis-read his works in order to find illustrations for their own theses. Anyone who reads Bergson fairly will have little difficulty in discovering that his so-called irrationalism is nothing more than a refusal to accept the reduction of the apprehension of the reality of a living being or of any living experience to concepts and conceptual knowledge. Concepts are part of knowledge, or of a given form of knowledge, but they are not the whole of knowledge. This is the extent of Bergson's claim, a claim which is supported by Kant, Hegel, Kierkegaard

21

and the existentialists, and by Husserl and phenomenalism. Intuition is, in everyday life, a rather pejorative notion, generally dismissed as being the so-called feminine alternative to intelligence and rationality; yet this notion of intuition as hunch, or as the little finger's whispering counsel about the future, is anything but a purely feminine prerogative.

Bergson's intuition is no substitute for dialectical reasoning and logic. Far from it; it is complementary to them as part of the most essential attribute of man which is reason. It is, as we shall see, something much akin to Coleridgean and Kantian imagination as the faculty which apprehends the wholeness and the true reality of things. By the end of the nineteenth century this faculty was granted very little scope in an epistemology which was dominated by positivism, utilitarianism, determinism, materialistic evolutionism and belief in the supreme value of science, summed up in Renan's words: 'One single belief reigns over these ruins, the belief in science, or better, the religion of science. . . . Faith in the future, faith in the infinite progress of the human spirit recorded by history will have as a final successful end, the complete emergence of God.' (Preface to *L'Avenir de la Science*, 1890) The emergence of God through science and through man! There lies the natural outcome of post-Kantian, post-Hegelian metaphysics, with their search for the absolute spirit, which Schopenhauer finds in the expression of the human will, and Nietzsche in the superman, creator of all values. The most important aspect of nineteenth-century thought, present in the most significant trends of philosophy, from Hegel to practically every other notable philosopher who came after him, with the exception of Kierkegaard, seems to be the growing tendency to replace God by man or to make of man the creator of God or even of Nature, as Fichte and Schelling put it. This growing anthropocentrism can be accounted for only by the development of science, which was bringing to man the hope that through science he would be able to achieve the dream of the millennium. The disillusion which followed the First World War and which is at the root of the rejection of reason by surrealism and the rejection of conceptualism by existentialism and phenomenalism, is the measure of the hopes which were placed on science and rationalism.

Bergson finds himself at the meeting point of two great streams of thought, each with deep roots in history, and each corresponding to deep social aspirations. On the one hand, there is the positivistic, materialistic, Spencerian evolutionism which captured Bergson's interest at the beginning of his life as a philosopher, and which goes back to Descartes' mechanistic view of the universe. On the other hand, there is the stream crystallised by Descartes' great contemporary Pascal, who contrasted *l'esprit de finesse*, otherwise called intuitive thought, with *l'esprit géométrique*, otherwise described as dialectical, logical reasoning, and who asserted that 'the heart has its reasons which reason does not know'. The heart, in this case, is consciousness, which is the basis of a kind of knowledge which completes that of the understanding. This line of thought is that of the French introspectives and moralists who range from Montaigne to Sartre and Gabriel Marcel, without forgetting of course Maine de Biran, to whom Bergson acknowledged an important debt, and Malebranche. Maine de Biran, a significant and wrongly neglected philosopher, restates in the early nineteenth century a conviction already well established in ancient Greece, that the search for truth lies inward, that man must look into himself, continuously endeavour to reach being which is part of Being, and act as mediator between God and Nature. In Bergson's time, Lachelier, Revaisson and Boutroux held similar views.

Bergson was deeply aware of the importance of science, and he never ceased to claim that his philosophising method was scientific. Gilbert Maire, one of his pupils, quotes an interview with him in which he says : 'Above all, do not neglect sciences. For philosophy as well as for them, there is only one authentic truth, and it is that achieved through experience.' (*Aux Marches de la Civilisation Occidentale*, Baudinière, 1929, p. 18) Further, in Maire's *Bergson mon Maître* (Grasset, p. 219), Bergson is quoted as saying : 'In a sense, if I may say so, any philosophy is only a succession of experiments.' Bergson acknowledges the fact that he was deeply impressed by Spencer's evolutionism, and that it was only after reading and re-reading him that he became dissatisfied and finally disappointed with the latter's treatment of the problem of time. Preoccupied as he was by this problem which is basic to human thought, he realised that mechanical time is not, properly speaking, time, but merely a sequence of unconnected moments, measured by a clock, which have nothing to do with the reality of human time which cannot be measured by such mechanistic means. He therefore set about rethinking this problem in terms different from Spencerian mechanism, and this thinking led him to the very heart of his philosophy, which, given his searches, is necessarily concerned with the nature of consciousness, with time as duration, and with the apprehension of this duration through intuition. That Bergson's work in this domain was of vital importance is confirmed by the views of one of the most important philosophers of his time, William James, who, after the publication of Bergson's *Matière et Mémoire* (1896), said: 'Like Berkeley's *Principles* or Kant's *Critique*, it creates a Copernican revolution, and it will open new grounds for philosophical discoveries.' And after the publication of *L'Evolution Créatrice* (1907) he said: 'Everything pales in the face of this divine apparition.' (*Correspondence*)

Bergson realised that one could not divide or fragment movement into a series of static points without landing oneself right in Zeno's paradox, that Achilles can never catch the tortoise. This is a distortion of the notion of movement which is thus reduced to a series of symbolic images drawn from its duration, while duration, the true movement itself, is ignored. This confuses, in fact, the *image* of movement—an imaginary line, a line supposedly left behind by the movement—with the *duration* of this movement which is not perceptible, but is apprehensible to consciousness, which seizes it in its true reality, concrete and qualitative, leaving out the spatial symbols placed between this true reality and ourselves. Philosophers, says Bergson, agree that there are two ways of knowing a given thing. One can either go around it or enter it. The first is relative, the second is absolute. This absolute is not the absolute in itself, that is to say the infinite, something which is not commensurate with the apprehending capacity of a finite existent, but the absolute in the sense that knowledge connects with the totality of the object. One has here the difference between knowledge through the understanding and the use of concepts and perceptions, and artistic knowledge through imagination which grasps the wholeness as well as the inner reality of the object of knowledge. To know truly something living and organic is to know it from the inside, and only the empathic coincidence of the subject with the object can give a total or absolute knowledge of this object. To know from the outside is to know relatively, that is to say in relation to the environment, to other things as parts of an intellectual composition. This kind of knowledge, useful though it is, can never lead to knowledge of the whole, for the whole is always more important than the elements which compose it and which are held together by an organic unity which can only be apprehended intuitively. The artists of the end of the nineteenth century and the beginning of the twentieth had, no doubt, become fully aware of this notion when they declared that all art aspires to music, that is to say to something apprehended as duration, or that the poem can only truly be apprehended as a whole and not as a series of analytical fragments, for, although one can go from the centre to the component parts, one cannot go from the parts to the organic whole. The conclusion of these views is that the poem is above all what it is, the experience that it suggests, and not what it says. The notion of a poem saying or narrating something was finally disposed of by *Symbolisme*, which is closely connected with English Romanticism. Romanticism had already anticipated the notion of the Bergsonian duration, of the inner *I* which transcends the individuated *I* and which lives and records the experience which is the poem while being wholly and entirely this experience and nothing else. From the Coleridgean notion of empathy to Blake's capacity to become the knot of wood which he contemplates, to Keats's negative capability and his idea of the poet-chameleon, or to Shelley's view of poetic inspiration as embers blown upon by all sorts of emotions, the concept of an *I* as a Cartesian *cogito*, which could organise and record, uninvolved, inner and outer reality, is as alien to English Romanticism as it is to Rousseau's day-dreaming.

Bergson stated his views about the relative and the absolute in an article entitled 'Introduction à la Metaphysique', which he published in 1903, and which later became part of *La Pensée et le Mouvant* published in 1934 and included in his *Oeuvres* (Presses Universitaires de France, 1959). It is from this edition that I quote : 'An absolute', he says, 'could be reached only through intuition, while everything else pertains to analysis. One calls intuition the "sympathy" thanks to which one transports oneself inside an object in order to coincide with what is unique in it, which consequently is inexpressible. Analysis is on the contrary the operation which reduces the object to already known elements, that is to say to elements which are common to this object as well as to others.' (*Op. cit.*, p. 1395) Intuition and sympathy seem to me to be what Coleridge defined respectively as imagination and empathy, while analysis is the work of the Lockian understanding which handles concepts, but which does not claim to be the whole of reason. This is a crucial point ever to be borne in mind, for all those who criticise Bergson as being irrational forget the fact that reason includes all the faculties that enable the human mind to know and to apprehend both the phenomenal world and the nature of its true self. Reason is what makes man, and it cannot be reduced to one of its component elements. The imagination is the capacity to enter into an object, to become aware of what it truly is, to apprehend its truth intuitively, and that really is *intelligere*, or to read inside. Therefore imagination is not opposed to intelligence but is a form of intelligence, and the most fundamental, for it is always this inside, the core or inner structure of anything, that matters most.

Bergson, who stated that he was only a metaphysician and nothing else, never saw any fundamental opposition between science and metaphysics. Although he deplored Kant's separation of practical from pure reason, he was aware that Kant had not attempted to do away with metaphysics; he had merely defined the domain in which metaphysics could operate with validity and contribute to human knowledge. Bergson, who quotes Berkeley's statement in the fourth dialogue of the *Alcyphron* that 'metaphysics is necessary to science because it teaches us to see behind the screen of reality', believed that metaphysics and science could work together towards the restoration of complete knowledge, and he believed that a precise, scientific knowledge of the facts is the prerequisite to the metaphysical intuition which penetrates to the heart of these facts. Metaphysics was for him the knowledge of true reality, which could neither be dissociated from phenomenal reality nor, of course, be looked upon as a résumé or synthesis of phenomenal knowledge. If he opposes the reduction of reason to the study of concepts and the workings of the understanding, he also opposes the reduction of metaphysics to the manipulations of abstract or Platonic ideas dissociated from reality. His aim is to go beyond concepts, to transcend them and to reach the inner reality which is not the eternal, motionless Idea of Plato, but the consciousness of self and the awareness of its true duration and of its relationship with being.

Bergson's first book, *Essai sur les Données Immédiates de la Conscience* (1889), comes to grips with the vital problem of the nature of the immediate or non-mediated *données* of consciousness, what he called *la durée* or duration. The *données* could be described as basic elements or foundations of consciousness, apprehended by consciousness, that is to say, in fact, consciousness apprehending its own reality. This reality is duration, and Bergson described it in the following terms : 'Pure duration is the shape taken by the succession of our states of consciousness when our inner *I* lets itself live, that is to say, when it abstains from establishing a separation between its present state and the preceding states.' (*Oeuvres, op. cit.*, p. 67) 'Duration takes the illusory form of an homogeneous milieu, and the link between these two notions—space and duration—is a simultaneity which could be defined as the intersection of time with space.' (*Ibid.*, p. 74) Space and time are reduced to an apprehension of the reality of the inner *I* as duration, something which is very close to the Kantian reduction of time and space to apprehensions of the inner *I*. With Kant, the pure intuition of space and time is a source of knowledge which produces absolute certainty. Bergson's idea of philosophy is in certain respects very traditionalist; it is, up to a point, that of Descartes. 'The philosophical method, as I understand it, is rigorously modelled on experience—internal and external—and does not make it possible to set forth any conclusion which is not absolutely in conformity with the empirical experience on which it is founded.' (Bergson, letter to Father de Tonquedec, 20th February, 1912) The empirical experience upon which truth rests is no longer mathematical, but biological, conforming with the fluctuations of life apprehended by consciousness. The apprehension of the inner states of consciousness is basically the apprehension of time, no longer mechanical time,

but true time which is beyond any kind of measurement or
divisions into past, present and future. Time is duration or the
intuitive awareness of consciousness apprehending itself both as
identical with itself and as continuously changing, in timeless
moments in which present and past and openness to the future
are unified in a mental representation. 'The crux of my views,'
says Bergson, 'is the intuition of duration,' and his conclusions
about duration are reached after a long examination of Zeno's
illusions about movement, an examination which seems to have
left its traces in Valéry's famous poem *Le Cimetière Marin*:

> Zénon! Cruel Zénon! Zénon d'Elée!
> M'as-tu percé de cette flèche ailée
> Qui vibre, vole, et qui ne vole pas!
> Le son m'enfante et la flèche me tue!
> Ah! le soleil . . . Quelle ombre de tortue
> Pour l'âme, Achille immobile à grands pas!
> (Paul Valéry: *Poésies,* Gallimard, 1942, p. 193)

From the problem of duration, Bergson passes to the problem
of free will and freedom, and here it must be said that his views
mark practically no progress on Kant's views, or on very orthodox Christian views, each naturally expressed in their own
respective terms. Bergson says: 'An act will be all the more free
that it tends to identify itself with the inner *I*.' (*Oeuvres, op. cit.*,
p. 110) 'We are free,' he continues, 'when our acts emanate from
our whole personality, when they express it and when they have
with it the indefinable resemblance which one finds between the
artist and his creation.' (*Ibid.*, p. 113) It seems to me that we
find ourselves confronted with the same intractable notions which
have always bedevilled the problem of freedom. How, for
instance, can one know what the inner *I* is, since this inner *I* is
not something static, but continuously changing and therefore
something which could have only a fleeting notion of what it was
before the act, which is described as free on the strength of its
conformity with it, has been performed? This act no doubt tells
us something about the true nature of the inner *I* that performed
it, but the inner *I* that performs this act and the one that was
going to perform it are not the same, and what the former one

was could be known only once the act, the freedom of which it is supposed to warrant, has been performed.

The same kind of criticism applies to the notion of personality which, as a continuous becoming, can never be used as a criterion or as a means of assessing the freedom of any action, since only the action gives an idea of what the performing personality is. The fact that, between the acting personality and his action, Bergson posits no more than the indefinable resemblance that exists between the artist and his creation, is quite significant, and at the same time in conformity with the truth, as well as with his notion of life and consciousness as continuous creation. Bergson illustrates this point by showing that Peter could not anticipate what Paul might do, unless he were exactly identical to Paul, something which is an obvious impossibility. Besides, the antecedents of any act cannot be known in advance since they are part of a vast unassessable number of potentialities; they can be assessed accurately only after this act has taken place. Until then, they are merely hypothetical possibilities or linguistic games in the conditional tense. Psychological motivations and causes cannot be examined diachronically; they are part of an aspect of synchronic time which is only ascertainable as duration, and therefore not measurable by scientific methods. Bergson's attempt to defend freedom on moral grounds is no less praiseworthy than that made by Sartre. Yet in both cases, logic is not on their side.

Leaving Sartre aside for the moment, it is, it seems to me, clear that Bergson has overlooked certain important aspects of the problem of freedom. First of all, to say that whatever happens must have causes is not the same thing as saying that the same causes produce the same effects. The first statement is an empirical and up to a point verifiable truth, the second is not so and carries with it very careful distinctions according to the domain in which it is applied. If the notion of a relation of causes to effects can be clearly established in the physical world and under laboratory conditions, it is not so in the field of psychology, for one can never exactly repeat states of consciousness. It seems to me therefore that Bergson's repudiation of psychological determinism is not quite supported by the evidence. Although the heterogeneity of states of consciousness cannot be mapped out and analysed with the rigour and certainty of the truth that prevails in the physical field, it is nevertheless a fact that whatever happens in consciousness is as necessarily caused or motivated as anything that happens in the physical world. Kant, who had not shaken himself free from the Cartesian-Platonic notion of a static Being, tried to avoid this difficult problem by positing a noumenal world and a phenomenal world, as if the twain could never meet; that is obviously an artificial division which can no longer be maintained. The point is that determinism in the sense of causality is not the same thing as predictability; neither can determinism be, on the psychological plane, the basis of the law that the same causes produce the same effects. Every psychological fact is, in some ways, unique, and therefore cannot be repeated by an attempt to reconstruct a background of causality which cannot be reconstructed, since one is dealing here not with mechanistic causality, but with creative causality. It is not a question of whether or not the same causes produce the same effects in all domains, but of acceptance of the undeniable fact, irrespective of the field concerned, that whatever is must have causes and therefore cannot be free, unless it is self-caused. This latter case could apply only to one single type of event or entity which would be the cause of all causes—the *ens summum*, the very principle of the life of the universe.

At the end of *Les Données Immédiates de la Conscience* Bergson asks two questions. The first is: is the definition of the free act that which consists in saying that it might not have been? This seems to be a strangely hypothetical way of approaching the problem of freedom, for it is evident that what has been obviously had to be, that is to say possessed enough positive causes or positive virtualities for being. This is neither determinism nor inflexible teleology, but, in the end, a mere question of greater probabilities in favour of being rather than not being. The second question is: shall we define the free act as that which could not be anticipated even if we knew in advance all conditions pertaining to it? This is, in fact, an idle question, for the conditions of an act do not exist complete, side by side with or apart from the act itself; they become what they are within the context of the act; above all, they can be known only once the act has taken place, and they therefore emerge as causes which have been transformed by actualisation and are only knowable as parts of this actualisation.

Matière et Mémoire (1896) begins with the words : 'This book asserts the reality of spirit and the reality of matter, and attempts to determine the relationship of one to the other by using a well defined example, that of memory. . . . It aims to attenuate considerably, if not to dispose of, the theoretical difficulties that dualism has always raised. . . .' (*Oeuvres, op. cit.*, p. 161) Bergson begins by repudiating absolute idealism, and by explaining that after Descartes' dualism, Berkeley, who had rightly ascertained the importance of secondary as well as primary qualities, could have solved the question of dualism if he had not gone too far into absolute idealism. Kant maintained the same type of dualism, which tended towards the abolition of metaphysics. Bergson, starting from psychology, wishes to restore its place to metaphysics, but he wishes to do so by showing himself faithful to scientific objectivity and to experience. The worth and vitality of a philosophical system depend, to a large extent, on its capacity to reflect the significant aspects of the life of its time and of life in general. Bergson's separation of matter from energy or spirit belongs to his time, or rather to the time when he wrote *Matière et Mémoire*, for very soon the physical sciences of the beginning of the twentieth century were going to show that one could no longer separate matter from energy and that these two notions were in fact interchangeable and practically one and the same thing.

Bergson's concern is with the relationship between consciousness and brain, the body and the outside world, perception and memory, psychology and physiology, and psychology and metaphysics. 'Psychology is', according to him, 'the study of the human mind working in the domain of practical reason, and metaphysics is this very same mind endeavouring to free itself from the conditions of useful action to apprehend itself as pure creative energy.' (*Ibid.*, p. 167) The problems which Bergson outlined occupy an important place in Sartrian existentialism and in the phenomenology of Merleau-Ponty who, in his book

Le Visible et l'Invisible, sought to deal with the question of the nature of the human body and its relationship with the outside world.

Bergson's two best known books are *L'Evolution Créatrice* (1907) and *Les Deux Sources de la Morale et de la Religion* (1932), with *Les Données Immédiates de la Conscience* not far behind. These three books are connected by themes which are worked out on different planes of human thought and activity, but which all centre around his main theme, the intuition of duration. William James, in a letter to his friend Schiller written on 15th June 1907, sets *L'Evolution Créatrice* in its true place in history. 'It is,' he says, 'a true miracle in the history of philosophy and as far as the content is concerned it marks, if I am not mistaken, the beginning of a new era; and as for the form, it has a note of persistent euphony. . . .'

Faithful to his belief in experimentalism, Bergson starts, in this book, with certain notions that explain some of the facts of evolution. He notes, for instance, that all things suggest an abundance or an explosion of forces which remain nevertheless complementary and maintain one broad, single direction. Is this fact merely mechanical, or is it due to some intelligence controlling and directing matter? The first case would presuppose pure mechanistic materialism, the second, finalism. Bergson excludes both, though it becomes more and more obvious, proceeding through *L'Evolution Créatrice*, that a certain amount of finalism remains but, as will be seen, of a very special type. Darwin thought that the various mutations that took place in life were due to small changes made by chance. Lamarck explained them as responses to environmental pressures and to functionalism; Bergson ascribes them to the resistance that matter opposes to the informing spirit which, from man onwards, becomes consciousness and, as Teilhard de Chardin was to agree later, makes of man the goal and the apex of evolution.

Mechanistic theories posit the possibility of knowing the future and the past by simply starting from the present. Since everything is mechanically connected and absolutely ineluctable in its unfolding, a supra-human mind could see the whole pattern

at one glance. Huxley puts the problem in a few brief remarks,
and Bergson thus quotes him : 'If the basic proposition of
evolution is true, that is to say if the whole world—organic and
inorganic—is the result of mutual interactions according to
definite laws and to forces inherent in the molecules which the
universe was originally composed of, the present world was
already part of the original cosmic haze, and an intelligence
strong enough to do so, and knowing the properties of the
molecule, could have anticipated the exact state of British fauna
in 1868, with as much certainty as one can predict what will
happen to human breath on a cold Winter day.' (*Ibid.*, p. 527)
This, as Bergson points out, implies a metaphysic according to
which the totality of the universe exists as a whole, in an eternal
present. But this is, in fact, a simplistic view, for although the
properties of the original molecules as they were five milliard
years ago may be known, the conditions in which these molecules
were to develop were continuously changing and consequently
having an influence on their behaviour. This influence would
necessarily play a part in their evolution without nevertheless
annihilating or destroying the basic properties which govern the
evolution of inorganic and organic matter and are part of its
own finality. Total mechanism, which implies the possibility of
knowing everything at once, pertains, like total finalism, to the
notion of fixed time, something that is, in fact, a denial of time;
it is simply time as Eternity, and of course total mechanism
implies finalism. But Bergson's view of time makes this type of
finalism unacceptable. 'There is,' he says, 'an internal finality;
everything is made for itself, and all its parts cohere for the
greater good of the whole and organise themselves intelligently
for this end.' (*Ibid.*, p. 529) Finality, to Bergson, is above all
identity of impulsion, but not a common aspiration of things
towards a given end, and this end of course cannot be known,
for 'life, though presented as harmonious, contains also many
discordances'. (*Ibid.*, p. 537) The theory of final causes goes too
far when it supposes that the future already exists in the present
as idea. Plato believed that to know the real was to find its
corresponding idea. This seems to me an incontrovertible truth,
for we can know the real only as mental substance—idea, concepts, perceptions. But the future is not made, it makes itself,

therefore it does not exist as idea; in fact the verb 'exist' is the wrong verb. The future does not exist at all in any shape or form, it is what will be; it is therefore the present about to become the past, it is the dream or the terror of this becoming, of the past pushing forward the present like rolling lava; it is both the freeing and the light of this lava, but it is not, it is going to be, and only once it is, will one know what it is, so that to be and to know are, if not synonymous for all forms of existence, certainly synonymous at the level where existence is conscious of being and connects with Being.

Bergson is neither a mechanist, nor a finalist, nor a vitalist. His dissatisfaction with Spencer's materialism, and his detachment from it, are due to the fact that he realised the limitations of any one of these three theories taken as a global explanation of the evolution of life. Nature is both orderly and disorderly, coherent and incoherent, brimming with bounty and fulfilment and displaying, at all levels of organic life, a continuous process of anthropophagy and destructiveness which, on the human plane, that is to say on the plane of life at the conscious level, exhibits the unbearable existence of evil, suffering and continuous dying. No Leibnizian or Christian explanation that the bad is part of the good, that evil is the price of freedom, or that disorder and suffering are not absolute, but merely the obverse, the dark shadows of the good, the true and the rational, can comfort man.

The notion of a set plan with a predetermined, fixed goal is logically untenable and, in fact, in the end, irreconcilable with the idea of God. As Bergson says: 'If evolution is continuous creation, it creates progressively not only the shapes of life but also the ideas that make it possible for intelligence to understand it and the terms that could be used to express it.' (*Ibid.*, p. 582) From the inorganic to the organic and to the emergence of consciousness, life seems to move towards a greater and greater comprehension of its true nature and of the direction of its development. What is therefore changing from the organic plane onwards, is the capacity of the nervous system of the animal world to develop until it can discover more and more of the laws that govern the life of the universe, and consequently of life itself. Life develops through the human organism the means by which it knows itself, and to know itself seems to be the finality of life. Life is therefore continuous creation along a broad direction which makes possible all sorts of abortive deviations, partial stops and periods of waste, but which nevertheless keeps to its broad direction towards self-knowledge. Bergson's main failure, due to the limitations of the physical knowledge of his time, is to talk about brute matter. Matter is not brute; matter is alive, and we are both matter and, of course, more than matter; matter being energy, we are energy understanding more and more what matter is. His mistake consists in positing some kind of separate spirit invading matter and shaping it, while matter as energy has in itself the forces, the appetitions and the laws that enable it to shape and complexify itself, towards greater and greater spiritualisation or undying energy.

Bergson says that according to Spencer, 'matter obeys its laws, that objects connect with objects, facts with facts through constant relationships, with consciousness receiving the imprint of these relationships and laws, thus adopting the general configuration of Nature and determining itself as intelligence.' (Ibid., p. 655) Bergson objects to this notion of intelligence which becomes thus an epiphenomenon of matter. He sees it, on the contrary, as a force or energy attuned to matter, inert matter which it can understand and explain, although by so doing it leaves out the living elements of matter which can be apprehended only by intuition. 'Intelligence and matter have adapted to each other not through any pre-established harmony, but progressively and naturally because it is the same inversion of the same movement which creates at the same time the intellectuality of spirit and the materiality of things.' (Ibid., p. 670) Intelligence and matter are both shaped by the force called élan vital, duration or life, and they have each their part to play. 'Intelligence as such is characterised by a natural incomprehension of life'* (ibid., p. 635), while instinct is connected with the very essence of life. Thus innate aspects of instinct bear upon things, the innate aspect of intelligence bears upon relationships, but instinct and intelligence complete each other. Intuition is instinct which has become disinterested and conscious of itself.

* Valéry echoes this with the words: 'Intelligence understands nothing of life.' (Idée Fixe, Gallimard, 1932, p. 98)

How intelligence, part of life, can be characterised by a natural incomprehension of life is difficult to understand; it is the word 'natural' which is puzzling, for it means, in the end, that life which is nature produces aspects of itself which are naturally unable to understand it. This is rather paradoxical, all the more so when a few pages later Bergson asserts that : 'Nature is one, and intelligence must apprehend it as a whole.' (*Ibid.*, p. 657) This seems to restore to intelligence practically the same function as to intuition, but the coincidence of the one with the other does not last, for the whole of Bergson's philosophy is shot through with various forms of dualism which only in rare moments resolve themselves into monism. We have matter and memory, the possible and the real, the continuous and the discontinuous, quality and quantity, instinct and intelligence, the open and the closed, life and matter. 'Life is movement and materiality is the opposite movement. . . . Life traverses matter and carves living being out of it.' (*Ibid.*, p. 707) This is, to say the least, a most curious notion of the relationship between an abstract force called life, and matter, and it posits of course a type of dualism and an impossible parallelism of these two aspects of life which are absurd at whatever level one might examine them. Whether one tries to think of their respective origins, or of the reason why there should be an interplay between the two, the result of which is life, it seems difficult to find any type of rational explanation.

'The *élan vital* consists in a compulsion to create, and it cannot create absolutely because it meets in front of itself matter, that is to say the movement opposed to its own.' (*Ibid.*, p. 708) The explanations that follow do not add to the clarity of these concepts. 'Consciousness or supra-consciousness is the origin of life . . . but this consciousness, which is an urge to create, only manifests itself when creation is possible.' (*Ibid.*, p. 716) This consciousness which is aware that creation is possible and knows when it is possible, maintains a form of dualism between the two component elements of creation that constitutes the most telling weakness of Bergson's philosophic system. This is fully illustrated in the chapter in *L'Evolution Créatrice* called 'Mechanism and Conceptualism', in which Bergson deals with what he calls illusions or false problems, and in which he endeavours to show that there is more in the idea of non-being than in that of being, more in the idea of the possible than in that of the real, more in that of disorder than in that of order, more in that of absence than in that of presence, etc. This seems to me a paradoxical way of approaching dualism, and a brief examination of two of these pairs of contrasted ideas should suffice to illustrate the sophistry of the argument. 'There is more', he says, 'in the idea of an object conceived as non-existent than in the idea of this same object conceived as existent.' (*Ibid.*, p. 737) First, one would need to know what the word 'more' applies to; more feelings perhaps, though even this is doubtful. But when Bergson says that there is more in non-being than in being, it is as if he said that there could be thought without existence. In order that the notion of non-being might be thinkable, there must first be being. Bergson asserts that men who ask the question: why being instead of non-being? imply that non-being has preceded being. The question: why being? means: what can be the reason why there is being instead of nothing? —but this 'nothing' is merely a notion thought of as the obverse of being, and not an entity preceding and being the cause of, or something more than, being. Being cannot come out of nothingness, and nothingness is not the negation of being, something that could make Bergson's conclusion possible. Nothingness or non-being cannot be more than being, because it is not, that is to say, it has no being, and having no being it could never cause or produce being. Non-being is a notion that can be thought of only by starting from being, and therefore as a quality or product of being but not as an *ens*. Non-being is what has no being and cannot on any account precede being, without making being impossible, that is to say unthinkable.

The notion that there is 'more in the idea of an object conceived as non-existent than in the idea of this same object conceived as existent', is obviously possible and entertainable if one knows the object, that is to say if the object either exists or is conceivable, and if the notion of 'more' is a psychological notion, a notion which is applied to feelings and to imagination; but to say that there is more in the possible than in the real is quite a different proposition, unless of course one confines oneself to a vague psychological domain of emotion, feelings and *rêverie*.

The Romantics well knew and loved this kind of state. The possible had always more attraction, more scope for the imagination than the real or action, thence the longings for the Rousseauesque *rêverie* of Saint-Preux, Werther, René. But if one moves out of the domain of speculation and applies these two notions—the possible and the real—to phenomenal reality, that is to say to what possesses objective existence, then one can see at once that 'possible' is only a word or a notion that could, of course, be submitted to the calculus of probabilities, but not something that could be known and therefore used as a mathematical notion described as containing more than another. The possible is the possible, and it can be known only as part of the real, that is to say only as a fraction of the notion destined to remain possible, therefore unknown. One can know only what has been actualised, what is real; and what could have been but has not been can never be known, and can only be in the end the object of verbal games. The possible which is known is reality projected into the past, for since the possible did not, properly speaking, exist before its actualisation, one could not know it before its actualisation had taken place. No doubt, a play like *Hamlet* or *Lear* was possible, in the sense that it is not possible to say that it was impossible, but that is about all that can be said, for *Hamlet*, as we know it, could only be what it is and have been written by the man Shakespeare, that is to say by a man possessing the genius, the sensibility, the intellect, experience and historical background of Shakespeare. The question as to whether another Shakespeare could have existed at any other time but the time when he existed, can only lead to the conclusion that if all the details which compose the portrait and above all the creations of Shakespeare have to be maintained, this hypothetical other Shakespeare would have had to be so perfect a replica of Shakespeare that he would necessarily be the same person, and nobody else, for it is philosophically accepted that there cannot be two absolutely identical things or persons.

Bergson is perfectly aware of the oneness of life, of the multiplicity of the One, and of the continuous interaction of the future with the present, and of the present with the past; he realises that the duality between Being and non-Being is not tenable, yet he is unwilling to accept the notion that existence cannot have begun at a certain moment in time, and that it must have possessed, from all eternity, the essence from which all things proceed to their logical existential shape. This notion excludes of course the interplay of efficient causality and free choice, and makes existence and whatever happens in it necessary, though of course unforeseeable. Bergson agrees in the sense that the absolute can only be equated with goodness and order, reveals itself near us, is, in a certain measure, in us, and is, by nature, psychological and not mathematical. We are part of the absolute, and, in fact, we participate in the making of the absolute and in the making of creation which is continuous and open. 'When we replace our being in our will and our will in the impulsion of which it is part, we realise that reality is continuous growth, a creation that continues without end. Our will already causes this miracle.' (*Ibid.*, p. 698) And a little later, after describing creation as a continuous flow in which things make and unmake themselves, he says : 'Provided I do not posit the centre [of this flow] as a thing, but as a continuity of projection, God, thus defined, stands for nothing already made. He is ceaseless life, action, freedom. Creation thus conceived is not a mystery; we experience it in ourselves the moment we act freely.' (*Ibid.*, p. 706) Our inner life helps us to grasp the true meaning of life, thence the importance of consciousness and consequently of psychology as a basis of metaphysical explorations.

Bergson's insistence on the importance of individual consciousness as the basis of truth connects with Kierkegaard, and acts as a link between him and the existentialists. In a direct intuitive way, which is the way to truth, Keats had put this point by saying that the real test of human truth is the human pulse. Bergson sees creation as continuous freedom and man himself as making or continuously creating himself through his freedom. This is, in some ways, very Sartrian, but with the difference that Bergson falls back on the old Kantian view of freedom which consists in saying that we are free when our true being connects with Being. But Kant made of freedom an emanation of the unfathomable noumenon, while Bergson, by positing a God continuously creating Himself, thus a God who is becoming, ignores the fact that this becoming cannot be freedom, but must be part of God's necessity. The notion of creation as a sower's gesture, or of life as struggling against matter which it endeavours to infuse with as much freedom as possible, is not tenable. This is in fact pure verbalism, for what is life if not creation, and creation cannot be the essence or origin of creation; neither could consciousness or supra-consciousness be the origin of life, since they are part of the growth and development of life. This separation of spirit or informing cause from matter is the main flaw of Bergsonism, a flaw which he tried to dispose of, though he was finally unsuccessful. The notion of consciousness as the principle of life had been anticipated by an American biologist, E. D. Cope, who stated his views in a book published in 1896 and entitled *The Primary Function of Organic Evolution*. On the other hand, Bergson's view that 'in the last resort man could very well be the *raison d'être* of the whole organisation of life on our planet' (*ibid.*, p. 652) anticipates Teilhard de Chardin.

It is only towards the end of his life, in his last full-length book, *Les Deux Sources de la Morale et de la Religion*, that Bergson succeeded in reducing dualism to monism, multiplicity of duration and consequently of Time, to one single universal Time—pure virtuality, simple totality of multiplicity, yet One, gathering up all durations. This is something different from Einsteinian time which admits a multiplicity of fields of observation, or systems in time, not a unified time, and is, therefore, as Bergson noted, a new way of spatialising time, and spatialised time was his life-long phobia. Bergson finally looked upon Time as continuous, while for Einstein there is a plurality of times which are each mathematically valid, according to their respective systems of reference, which imply their positions in space and in Time, or the fourth dimension called space-time. For Bergson, time, the *élan vital*—duration—is life dividing itself into its multiple forms.

These conclusions were not reached easily, and *La Pensée et le Mouvant*, published in 1934, is above all the record of these hesitations and explorations carried out over thirty years, since some of the essays it contains were published in 1903. Bergson's first philosophical meditations led him to the conclusion that time had always been dealt with in terms of space, so that time and space had become interchangeable. He soon realised that this spatialisation of time could not apply to the inner life of consciousness, in which time could be neither fragmented nor localised in space, since it was a continuous, uninterrupted flow which he called duration. The understanding, which Bergson wrongly described as intelligence, can apprehend time as conceptualised space, or as extension or secondary qualities of things, but it cannot apprehend time as movement or duration. This only intuition can do, because it does not attempt to apprehend the whole as a concept, but apprehends its individual parts in their unity which is their inner duration. 'Intuition means therefore immediate consciousness, vision which hardly distinguishes itself from the object seen, knowledge which is contact and even coincidence with this object.' (Oeuvres, op. cit., p. 1273) This means, in fact, the apprehension through individuated essence of the essence of an object or the experience of this essence. In his famous essay *Introduction à la Métaphysique* which is part of this volume and which contains many of the seminal ideas that he developed later, he says: 'There are two ways of knowing a thing; the first turns around it, the second gets into it; the first type of knowledge is relative, the second absolute.' (*Ibid.*, p. 1393) The notion of absolute is here equated with simplicity or oneness and indivisibility, and it can only be reached through intuition, while relative knowledge is a matter of analysis and accumulation of qualities and concepts. 'We call intuition the "sympathy" through which one transports oneself inside an object in order to coincide with it; it is unique and consequently inexpressible.' (*Ibid.*, p. 1395) This faculty Blake, Coleridge and the Romantics called imagination, and imagination, part of reason, unifies the various aspects of the apprehension of reality through images. The reality that we seize through intuition is the reality of our inner self flowing through time, making time. No two moments are the same; there is no past trailing behind us, with 'us' being some kind of imaginary entity which is able to move forward, when summoned, from one given point to another. There is only a continuous living light called consciousness, and this indefinable, continuously changing light contains within it, ever present, all the accretions of its past states, which can be neither rolled back nor ignored, and which constitute a more or less ever-moving whole which is only finally transformed and fixed by its passage through what Mallarmé called 'ce peu profond ruisseau, calomnié, la mort'.

Our inner life is therefore both most complex and varied, and above all difficult to grasp in terms of concepts that would turn it into abstract terminology and consequently empty it of its true substance and make of it a kind of dead butterfly under glass; its colours and shape would still be there, but the life and movement that made its dance possible would have gone; and in life as well as in art the dance is all. Only concrete images can suggest the reality of the intuition of duration; they are not a reconstructed representation of the object by the understanding, but symbolic entities to be used by the intuition of the reader or onlooker to recapture the original duration that created them. This is in fact the basic principle of art as source of inspiration and radio-active material for the apprehending imagination, and not as conceptualised, analysed, fully digested material to be absorbed by the reader's or listener's mind. Analytical, dialectical knowledge is applicable to science, to most aspects of philosophy, including metaphysics, and also to some aspects, though not all, of art and religion, the final truth of which rests upon intuition, that is to say upon the capacity of placing oneself, through imagination, at the heart of things. 'Internal duration is the continuous life of a memory that prolongs the past into the present, whether the present contains a clear, ceaselessly growing image of the past or whether it rather testifies, through its continuous change of quality, to the ever increasing load that becomes heavier the older we grow. Without this survival of the past into the present, there would be no duration, there would only be instantaneity.' (*Ibid.*, p. 1411) This internal duration is memory; creation in art is the capacity to connect individual memory with the cosmic memory, the vast Jungian subconscious, the *anima mundi* of Yeats, or with Being which is the subsistence of being.

The real, the living, the concrete are varied and changing and cannot be reduced to analyses which fragment and freeze them into set patterns. A poem, for instance, is a whole and not a sum of analyses, and one cannot pass from analysis to intuition; one must begin, in this case, with intuition. Movement in space is always discontinuous, it is always a series of changing positions which are held together by the mind. The various positions of a mobile are merely points in space conceived as the substratum of the movement; this substratum is purely imaginary and not real. Concepts are of exactly the same nature as the imaginary points of the movement; they are the qualities of a given object, while the inner life of movement is absent. Thus concepts cannot penetrate to the heart of the real, and the mistake consists in believing that knowledge starts from fixed concepts and that with them one can know and understand moving reality. 'That is why', says Bergson, 'we so often take the logical apparatus of science for science itself, forgetting the intuition from which the rest may have emerged.' (*Ibid.*, p. 1423)

The claims that Bergson makes for intuition are neither exclusive nor absolute. He is pre-eminently concerned with the fact that Kant, by upholding the doctrine that we do not possess a faculty of intellectual intuition (as Descartes believed), had made our concepts empty or analytic, unless they were the results of our pure intuition of space and time. By so doing, he had reduced science to relationships between existing concepts, and metaphysics to artificiality. Bergson is concerned to point out that living reality is continuously changing and can be apprehended only by intuition. The living is what changes, as Valéry said:

> Beau ciel, vrai ciel, regarde-moi qui change!
> Après tant d'orgueil, après tant d'étrange
> Oisiveté, mais pleine de pouvoir,
> Je m'abandonne à ce brillant espace . . .

(*Poésies*, Gallimard, 1942, p. 189)

Les Deux Sources de la Morale et de la Religion (1932), one of Bergson's most important works, sums up his philosophy by applying his famous concepts of 'open' and 'closed', relative and absolute, human and abstract, to morality and religion, and by offering an explanation of the true meaning of creative evolution or *élan vital*, source of life. This much admired book has also been much misunderstood and often used as a means to castigate Bergson as an anti-rationalist, a charge completely unsupported by the evidence of his writings. Bergson never proposed a distinction between closed and open rationalism, because such a notion was not part of his thinking; he proposed a distinction between closed and open morality, and closed and open religion, a very different matter. He begins by stating the Aristotelian truth that man is a political animal, and that neither Robinson on his island nor Kipling's lonely forester ever forgot society. Man is man, not in isolation but as a social animal, yet society must not be equated with humankind, for to do so would be to equate the part with the whole. Society with its laws, its habits, its customs, its desire for self-preservation, its imitations of the natural order, is a closed world. Humankind is an organic entity, pervaded with natural and even transcendental laws embracing all men, and is therefore continuously open to change.

Bergson applies to morality the same criteria as to intuition and intelligence or understanding. Intuition applies to movement, and intelligence to immobility. Open morality implies movement, closed morality implies immobility. Whether of social or anthropomorphic origin, whether created by design or born purely by accident, religion is a necessary part of social life. Western society rests above all upon various forms of religious thought. For a while, this society hesitated between Socrates and Christ, for the doctrines created by these two men, as well as the two men who preached them, were extremely close, and both men accepted death for the beliefs they preached and put into practice. Socrates identified knowledge with goodness and with virtue. He established the pre-eminence of reason, and Western rationalism flows from him. His mission, like that of Christ, was both religious and mystical, and like Christ, he preached and lived his philosophy but did not write it down. He left that to others. He was the great teacher, and his supra-rationalism reached beyond reason, and joined Christ's all-embracing love of mankind and faith in divine justice. He wanted to change society but he did not want to overthrow it; he accepted the obligations and the laws of his society and he was prepared to die to show his respect for them. Christ was an outsider to the society in which he was born, and his teaching implied a total transformation of this society, and the creation of a new one.

Great leaders, saints or mystics, whether they are called Socrates or Christ, are means by which societies open themselves to creativity and take a leap forward in morality as well as in religion. They represent what is best in mankind; they are its true creativity, and their call and example are never forgotten. They break out of the system or order based on impersonal obligations, which is the hallmark of the closed society, and they appeal to the individual conscience to listen to itself and to find in itself the echo of their preaching which connects it with true Being. And here it is necessary to quote Bergson to show how he differentiates between certain forms of the intellect and emotion : 'The obligation which is connected with order is, in as far as it is original and fundamental, supra-intellectual. The efficiency of its appeal rests upon the power of the emotion which caused it, which is still there or could be there, if only because it can be turned into idea and is also more than idea; it is supra-intellectual. The two forces acting in different areas of the soul project themselves onto the immediate plane which is that of intelligence. They will henceforth be replaced by their projections which intermingle and interpenetrate each other. The result is a transposition of orders and appeals in terms of pure reason. Justice is thus continuously enlarged by charity, and charity takes more and more the form of simple justice. . . . Moral life will be a rational life.' (*Ibid.*, pp. 1046–47)

This quotation contains two important aspects of Bergson's thought. First the idea that emotion is the basis of morality, and that this emotion connects morality not only with obligation but, above all, with justice and charity, and thus makes it worthy of human kind. The emotion that does this is creative emotion which works through privileged beings, in order to outline the pattern of the open society, a society of creative minds. The great leaders of human kind, says Bergson, who have broken through the barriers of the city, seem by so doing to have installed themselves within the direction followed by the *élan vital.* There is obviously something Hegelian in the thought expressed here; it is not quite the hero as incarnation of the *Zeitgeist*, working for the advent of the absolute, but it certainly is the hero or genius working in order to reveal to mankind the spirit or direction which informs it.

The second important aspect of Bergson's thought that must be briefly examined here is the meaning he commonly gives to the word 'intelligence'. There are very many aspects and various levels of the faculty broadly described as intelligence; there is a level at which Bergson equates intelligence with reason; here, intelligence is logos, that is to say the faculty that truly makes man. But it is not this highest form, or this supreme aspect, of intelligence or reason which Bergson criticises, but reason reduced to abstract, dehumanised logic. Bergson does not confuse intellect and intelligence, intellectualism and rationalism. For him the understanding, which is more or less what he calls intellect, deals with the logical obligations of social laws necessary to morality, and he acknowledges that they are necessities inherent in evolution, parts of the evolution of life, which only integrated reason apprehends, even when they belong to the supra-intellectual level or to what Kant describes as the domain of speculative reason, that is to say the domain of the ideas that are the very structures of reason. Bergson is, if one wishes to simplify, anti-intellectualist, but not anti-rational. Like Whitehead, he abhors what the latter called 'one-eyed reason', but he constantly upholds the importance of integrated reason which necessarily includes intuition or imagination. It is noteworthy that a great mind like Bertrand Russell always refused to be described as an intellectual. There is indeed something arid and restrictive in the meaning of the word 'intellect' or 'intellectual'.

For Bergson it is intelligence or reason that has enabled man to separate himself from the animal world and to organise himself into societies of greater and greater complexity. But man's progress would have been limited had it not been for the emergence every now and then, here and there, of men of genius who reveal to human consciousness the unforeseen, untapped forces which transcend the group or the society and the time to which they belong, and appeal to the whole of mankind. These geniuses, whatever the domain in which they operate, mark significant moments reached by human evolution, and they all represent an original aspect of the true love of mankind, which seems to be the very essence of their creative force. The creative

emotion of these privileged or elect incarnations of life affects
the whole and nourishes its growth, both directly and mnemoni-
cally, when men revive or rekindle this original emotion by
bringing the past back into the present. These incarnations are
not chosen by any imaginary overseer of the unfolding of
evolution; they simply are, just like volcanoes on the earth; they
happen to be in certain places, they erupt at certain moments,
and they are in a sense irrational, that is to say opposed to the
order of the day and of the city in which they live. They have
to be so in order to break the established order, which, for those
who control it, is obviously rational, that is to say in conformity
with the predominant views of the society which they rule, but
they are as much a necessary part of the unfolding of history
and creation as volcanoes are part of the life of the earth. These
men of vision, whether they are called Buddha, Socrates, Christ,
Mohammed, Gandhi, embody emotional forces which cannot
be replaced by the notion of *L'Etre Suprême* or by that of the
spirit of science. They are not abstractions, they are concrete
human emotions which clearly show that abstract, logical thinking not only is not enough, but can be desiccating, withering
and destructive to mankind, unless it is always infused with the
great principles of love, charity and compassion for all men.
These three vital aspects of the life of man do not surge from
the intellect, they surge from the imagination or from what
Bergson calls intuition. Bergson sees social pressures and obligations, and the creative emotions or manifestations of love
which every now and then reshape and revivify them, as complementary aspects of life; the former are intent upon preserving
the established social situation, and the latter are intent upon
transfiguring it every now and then, through individuals acting
as genetic mutations which renew the strength of creative
evolution. At all levels, Bergson maintains, therefore, the
principle of duality in oneness which is the oneness of integrated
reason.

Religion and morality are for Bergson complementary; one
needs the other; and in primitive society morality is co-extensive
with religion 'which is a defensive reaction of Nature against the
representation by intelligence of the inevitability of death'. (*Ibid.*,
p. 1086) Thence the notion of the immortal soul, a phantasmal

projection of the body, part of the spirit of life, continuously active in it, so as to make everything understandable. The primitive mind knows no notion of chance; there is a spirit in everything, and from spirits to gods, and then to the personalising of these gods, the transition is easy and understandable. Religion reinforces the social order : 'It is a defensive reaction of Nature against what might be depressing for the individual and destructive for society in the exercise of intelligence.' (*Ibid.*, p. 1150) But religion and morality are not the same; far from it; the ancient gods behaved as they pleased, and Christian religion has throughout the centuries condemned behaviour that society allowed. Still, society and religion need each other; the one has helped to confirm the customs and traditions that form the basis of the other; both naturally tend to staticity or closedness, and both distrust intelligence which analyses and questions and is an obstacle to serenity and staticity, and needs to return to its origins and to rediscover its connections with the wholeness of life : 'But we know that there exists around intelligence a vague and evanescent fringe of intuition. Could this fringe not be fixed and intensified, and above all, could it not be completed in action, for it only becomes pure vision through the weakening of its essence, or if one might put it so, through an abstraction practised upon itself.' (*Ibid.*, p. 1155) This clearly shows that for Bergson intelligence and vision are one in their essence, and the essence in question is clearly part of the essence of Being, cause of life. A human being capable of connecting with this essence would feel in himself immense power, and 'his attachment to life would henceforth be inseparable from this principle or essence which is joy within joy and love of what is only love'. (*Ibid.*, p. 1155) This is the language of the mystics, of St John of the Cross and St Teresa of Avila, the language of Christ as well as of the *Song of Songs*.

Mysticism, which is not to be confused with myth-making, connects individuated being with the *élan vital* or true being, and is very rare. If all men or most men could share in the strength of the few extraordinary men capable of mysticism, then the life of mankind would be different, then men would hear the true voice of mankind and be inspired by their glimpses of the new worlds which through love they could reach. Then wars would be abolished, and society and religion, instead of being locked up in self-interest and the desire to cling to what they possess, would be open and dynamic, in a constant state of transformation, therefore truly living, and not more dead than alive. This would not be disorder, but order, order of a higher kind, yet part of reality, so that there would be no conflict between intuition and rationalism. Mysticism is transcended reality; it is not wild fantasy. The great mystics have aimed at transforming the world, and not at going to the moon or Mars. Their aim was the true heart of man, and the means to connect this true heart with being. The Greeks, founders of rationalism, were both rationalists and mystics. Mysticism is not irrational, it is complementary to reason, and part of unfathomed aspects of reason, for it is part of man's ways of reaching beyond his individuated essence and connecting with the essence of being or with the creativity of life. Mysticism provides a form of knowledge that cannot be obtained through analysis, or through inductive or deductive processes. It cannot be scientifically ascertained or anticipated, but it can be verified by experience, through the ways in which it shapes human life and history. It can be assessed only through its effects, and the effects of this knowledge, far from being opposed to science, on the contrary provide science with the ideal of discovering means of showing a greater and greater love of man to man. Pasteur was moved by such an ideal, which obviously differs from that which led to the making of the Hiroshima bomb.

All the great faiths of the world come from great mystics and are the results of mystical experiences, of nights of the soul, or of long meditations in darkness, in deserts or on mountains. Even Buddhism is based on the revelation that Buddha had under his bho tree. Its message transcends the world of reason, and if it does not call forth the love of action in order to spread love, it preaches charity, the absolute respect for life at all levels, and constant efforts to reach the world of spirit and non-action. Marxism is certainly no mysticism, but there is at its root a vision, an earthly vision admittedly, of the city of God, and a messianism which, in its most elevated form, that is to say in the form which aims at the betterment of man without any cruelty or suffering imposed on other men, is one of the crying needs of mankind. But alas, its earthly application has been, until now, stained by a violence that is alien to the love of man. 'When the depths of the soul,' says Bergson, 'are stirred, what emerges on the surface and reaches consciousness takes the shape of an image or an emotion.' (*Ibid.*, p. 1170) The soul in this state feels in the presence of a vision that gives it life. Thence illumination, ecstasy and total oblivion of time in a joy without bounds. This experience, which raises the individual to the level of the divine, brings only humility, since as a believer he is deeply aware that God or the Divine has consented to lower Himself to his level. This is the opposite experience to that of those possessed by evil, who are convinced that their powers have raised them to the level of the Divine or the absolute. For the mystic, the love that henceforth he has in him is not only the love of God but the love of all men; this love is, above all, meta-physical, and its aim is to complete, with God's help, God's creation. Mysticism is the incandescent flame or lava that over-flows the fixed channels of the established churches or religions and sets them alight or opens them, not to destroy them but to restore to them their pristine, active roles as agents of the Divine. Mysticism and Christianity are part of each other, and one could not exist without the other. The mystics continue Christ, and their immersion in or contact with Being translates itself into action in life, and not into withdrawal from life. 'The mystics,' says Bergson, 'unanimously testify that God needs us as we need Him . . . in order to love us. Such will be the conclusion of the philosopher who studies mystical experience, and creation will appear to him as God's enterprise to create creators and to surround Himself with beings worthy of His love.' (*Ibid.*, p. 1192)

Life, according to Bergson, must exist on other planets also, and as far as the earth is concerned, he says that though life was not predetermined, it certainly was not an accident, and he adds : 'We have shown, on the contrary, that matter and life as we define them are given together, as interdependent.' (*Ibid.*, p. 1192) And he continues in terms that illustrate this inter-dependence between matter and life and between the human being and the universe of which he is an integral part. 'The vital current which traverses matter and which is probably its *raison d'être*, we shall take simply as given. . . . Living beings have been called to existence because they were destined to be loved and to love, and creative energy is defined by love. . . . Separated from God who is this very energy, they could only appear in and be part of a universe, and that is why the universe has emerged.' (*Ibid.*, p. 1194) This excludes all ethical connotations and makes it clear that the creative energy which informs matter is necessarily harmonised with it and complementary to it. The equation of creative energy with love could present difficulties if one allowed the word 'love' any other meaning except that of the appetitions and attractions that preside over the organisation of the atoms of matter. This meaning, which makes life possible, places true creativeness beyond any notion of good and evil, predetermination or finality, on the level where it belongs, which is that at which matter and energy are inseparable and contain elements and qualities that make possible their inorganic and organic aggregates into more and more complex, interconnected patterns which make up a coherent whole called life.

Bergson's words correspond to the views of Teilhard de Chardin : 'For if our body is matter to which our consciousness applies itself, it is coextensive with our consciousness, and comprises everything we perceive; it reaches as far as the stars.' (*Ibid.*, p. 1194) If body and consciousness are coextensive and cannot be separated, neither can the human body be separated from the universe to which it belongs, which, far from crushing it by its infinity, as Pascal felt, is the domain in which it operates, and is as important a field for consciousness as the human body itself. It is not only the human body that is part of nature; intelligence itself, part of the body, is also part of nature. This is a most important point, to be strongly underlined, for Bergson has often been wrongly accused of setting intelligence against nature. Bergson sees intelligence as part of nature, having, like instinct, its part to play in the natural harmony of the universe : 'A body which comprises constructive intelligence, carrying around itself a fringe of intuition, is the most complete achievement of Nature.' (*Ibid.*, p. 1241) This would seem to be the aim of the evolution of life; but this aim has now been forgotten by intelligence divorced from intuition which has, through science, practically mastered all aspects of matter. We are on the threshold of new worlds, and Bergson concludes with the words: 'Mankind must ask itself if it wishes to continue to live, and if so, it must ask itself whether it is prepared to make the necessary effort so that even on our rebellious planet, the universe might carry out its essential function which consists in being a machine to make gods.' (*Ibid.*, p. 1245)

A few years after this Bergsonian conclusion, Teilhard de Chardin talked of the noosphere or of the spiritualisation of life, and J.-P. Sartre asserted that man's dream is to make himself God. There is no great distance between some of Bergson's views and existentialism, and it is quite understandable that it should be so, for nothing is ever new, everything is continuation, and the ethos of the age of Bergson is not very different from that of the age of Sartre. Some aspects of man's decadence and of the disintegration of spirit, something that could be described as dehumanisation, have increased to the point where man's true face has practically disappeared under the distorted mask that covers it. I should never dream of calling this, as some do, an animal mask, for the animals give us daily lessons in affectionate, brotherly behaviour, and when they perform some cruel act, their doing so is simply part of the inflexible geometry of their instinct and not the result of debased reason, which man uses not in order to ennoble his image but merely to force down his victim's throat specious, egotistical explanations—the vinegar-filled sponge in the mouth of suffering Christ. Bergson, a wandering Jew on the verge of Christianity, yet deeply conscious of his growing solidarity with his persecuted brothers whose Calvary was already looming on the horizon of his declining years, had foreseen the collapse of barren reason and the logic with which so-called Aryans were to justify their crimes, tyrants their oppressions, and high-minded Christians their destruction of poor black- or yellow-skinned peoples standing in the way of their march towards economic control of the earth.

It is, above all, this type of intellectualism—dweller in dry skulls, without any connection with the heart, its generous impulses and its wide-ranging vision of more humane mankind —that Bergson condemns. It is man living only by customs, habits, regulations, in walled cities, and wrapped up in dogma-ridden religion and morality, that he repudiates, and not true religion, Christ-born morality, or reason as living, transforming *logos*. Those who, like Julien Benda, wish to make of him the scapegoat for the irrationalism of his time, ignore the fact that from Dostoyevsky to Nietzsche, Kafka, Mallarmé, Valéry, Claudel, Bradley, Eliot, Braque or Picasso, all the great thinkers and artists of his time understood and condemned, as he did, the transformation of ethical and religious values into mere habits or empty gestures used as cloaks to hide the callousness and total indifference to suffering and poverty of so-called rational and orderly societies. Men of vision, whether scientists or artists, could neither fail to apprehend the true reality of things nor ignore it. So they all despised this travesty of reason, this pretence of objectivity, and they turned for truth, not towards shallow political puppets or religious leaders, but towards their inner selves, with the conviction that truth could come only from the heart and the mind of the searcher. The artist made of his truth the one and only proof and awareness of his own existence, and in a world without God, or with God in abeyance, he sought God not in empty churches but in himself.

Truth is therefore the inner self apprehending itself in the act of knowing itself and thus of being. Bergson's 'duration' is not very different from that of Valéry in *Le Cimetière Marin*, *La Jeune Parque* and *Mon Faust*, or that of Claudel, Gide or Proust. Truth is, as Kierkegaard had already said, truth lived, or reached through the leap into faith, or into memory and its sea of vague sensations and nothingness from which Valéry, Proust or Gide extract, in the wake of Rousseau, the awareness of existence. Bergson extracts his duration from the past which is a kind of ontological memory containing particulars and universals, coextensive with the present, which never is, since it is always passing, always becoming the past, which thus is always both the present and the future. The present was, and will be, but never is, it is always what it is not. Poets have also expressed this in their different ways. Eliot, in *Burnt Norton* (*Four Quartets*), said:

Time present and time past
Are both perhaps present in time future,
And time future contained in time past.

And Eugene O'Neill, through Mary Tyrone in *Long Day's
Journey into Night*, said: 'The past is the present; isn't it? It's
the future too, we all try to lie out of that but life won't let us.'
The intuition or awareness of duration is therefore the awareness
of both existence and continuous becoming, an awareness which,
it seems to me, precludes any division, any notion of *in se* and
per se. The awareness of duration is one, and is always present
and indivisible, irreducible to spatialisation or the fragmentation
of time into instants. It is the continuously moving, merging
point of past and present. This duration, the apprehension of the
inner self as uninterrupted, ever-flowing time, has, of course,
various levels of consciousness or intensity, but all these levels of
consciousness or intensity are canalised into the central flux
which is the inner self and which connects the multiplicity of
selves as individuated beings with the One or with Being, which
for the believer, like Claudel, is God. There is only one time,
impersonal time which gathers up all, said Bergson in *Les Deux
Sources de la Morale et de la Religion*; and Valéry, in *Ebauche
d'un Serpent*, said that God reduces Himself to Oneness:

> Il se fit Celui qui dissipe
> En conséquences, son Principe,
> En étoiles, son Unité.

(Poésies, p. 170)

Valéry is in many ways Bergsonian, and the main theme of
his poetry is the birth of consciousness or the nature of creativity.
His aim is the intuitive apprehension of the duration that corresponds to the hesitations between being and non-being, that
is to say the coming to life of the act of creativity, and its
representation in concrete images drawn from memory and held
together by a sustained rhythm and by imaginative control of
the whole poetic experience in a living, symbolic entity which
can henceforth be used by other human beings as a starting point

to recapture, each in his own terms, the duration that lies at its heart. The Valérian journey is always an awakening and a progression from chaos and non-being to being, or from hesitations and negations of being to an affirmation of being, as asserted at the end of *Le Cimetière Marin* :

> Le vent se lève!... il faut tenter de vivre!

> *(Poésies,* p. 194)

or of *La Jeune Parque* :

> Alors, malgré moi-même, il le faut, ô Soleil,
> Que j'adore mon coeur où tu te viens connaître,
> Doux et puissant retour du délice de naître,
> Feu vers qui se soulève une vierge de sang
> Sous les espèces d'or d'un sein reconnaissant!

> *(Poésies,* p. 106)

Being is change and death; to live is to die. Creativity and consciousness, through action and language, imply a struggle, a negation of the pleasurable side of non-consciousness and non-awareness of being, as expressed in *La Pythie* :

> Mais enfin le ciel se déclare!
> L'oreille du pontife hilare
> S'aventure vers le futur.
> . . .
> Honneur des Hommes, Saint LANGAGE,
> Discours prophétique et paré,
> Belles chaînes en qui s'engage
> Le dieu dans la chair égaré,
> Illumination, largesse!

> *(Poésies,* p. 160)

But in the end, the poetry of Valéry, from *Charmes* to *Mon Faust*'s most important words, is an affirmation of willed existence and duration against negativity and nihilism : 'Je vis. Et je ne fais que vivre. Voilà une oeuvre. . . . Je nais de chaque instant pour chaque instant. VIVRE ! . . . JE RESPIRE. N'est-ce pas tout? JE RESPIRE. . . . J'ouvre profondément chaque fois, toujours pour la première fois, ces ailes intérieures qui battent le temps vrai. Elles portent celui qui est, de celui qui fut à celui qui va être . . . JE SUIS, n'est-ce pas extraordinaire? Se soutenir au-dessus de la mort comme une pierre se soutiendrait dans l'espace? Cela est incroyable. . . .' (*Mon Faust*, Gallimard, 1946, pp. 95–97)

Valéry's thought is not concerned with denials or denigrations of reason or with attempts to universalise his poetic experiences. He knows, as every poet knows, that every experience is unique, and he is too Bergsonian to ignore the fact that duration also is unique, for if it were not so, it would be a concept and no longer a living reality. His concern is the capacity of the mind to keep itself constantly open to all possibilities and to test their capacities for actualisation. It is a kind of identification of the function of the mind with that of life itself. The great man for him is Da Vinci, he who can turn the attention of his mind to any problem and attempt to solve it. The mind or reason must be kept in a constant state of readiness, and readiness is all. Again this attitude links with Bergson's view that there is more in the negation of a thing than in the thing itself. Yet in the end Valéry always accepted the triumph of the senses and of material life over the pure Mallarméan abstraction. Far from him the dream of producing an 'Orphic explanation of the earth'; *La Jeune Parque, Le Cimetière Marin* and *Mon Faust* end with an acceptance and an assertion of the importance of existence which is quite Claudelian. Claudel had no such doubts or hesitations; the universe God made, sustained by God's presence, ever reveals itself to man 'fresh as on the first dawn'. 'With each breath the world is as new as at the first breath of life that filled the lungs of the first man.' (*Art Poétique*, Gallimard, 1903, p. 45)

The age of Valéry, Claudel, Proust, Gide and Bergson had repudiated Baudelaire's Parnassian notion : 'Je hais le mouvement qui déplace les lignes'; movement and change were in fact the essence of life and the basic elements of psychological assessments and researches. Painters tried to suggest movement in painting by applying photographic processes conveying depth and a new perspective. The futurists declared that a racing car was more beautiful than the *Victory* of Samothrace, and they decomposed and recomposed objects, not according to rational perceptions, but, like the Cubist painters, according to their subjectivity and their intuition of the reality of things. The Surrealists and Dadaists, contemporary with Bergson and Freud, sought to liberate the subconscious and the world of dreams as the source of art. What they all rejected, and what the two most brutal wars of all time have rejected, is the now untenable notion of a highly controlled Cartesian man perfectly conscious of the mechanism and import of all his actions. It has become clear that man is dominated by emotions and instincts which, far from being life-bent, have been distorted or camouflaged under a veneer of rationalisations and given, through techniques developed by reason, the means to be indulged in with unparalleled ferocity. Artists and philosophers, attuned to wavelengths different from those of their average fellow beings, have grown more and more aware of the gap between professed ideals and the sordidness and cruelty of human life, and like Bergson or Whitehead, they have refused to accept the dictates of 'one-eyed reason', and sought for answers capable of expressing the true reality and individuality of human experience.

Living in an age when even poets could not help paying homage to science, Bergson looked upon philosophy as a true science, as starting from facts given by experience, its goal being the real, its main virtue humility, its worth its capacity to reflect aspects of our life or of life in general. Yet science deals with universals and with knowledge through concepts and not with particulars or with the becoming of human experience; so that however scientific and objective the observation of this becoming may be, the becoming itself, because of its uniqueness, eludes scientific measurement. Concepts are necessarily external to the uniqueness of individuated experience, and if the mind wishes to try to know such experience through concepts, it has to move from the contrasting and varied abstractions resulting from external analyses, towards the internal movement or change that is the cause or origin of these abstractions, and that, as movement, tends towards the transcendence of contrasts and oppositions to reach a final oneness or unity, analogous to the

Hegelian oneness of spirit. This movement can be seized only by intuition which, as Bergson pointed out, hovers on the fringes of intelligence, and if instead of 'intelligence' he had used the word 'understanding', 'intelligence' would then have been equated with 'reason', and a good deal of unnecessary carping concerning Bergson's philosophy would have been avoided.

This was the Kantian distinction between intuition and intellect that Bergson as a post-Kantian failed to make, in spite of the fact that Kant was constantly present in his mind as an inspiration, or as a basis of some of his definitions, the most important being those concerning intuition. For Kant, all intuitions are from the senses, therefore concerned with space and time which they incorporate in themselves. There is no possibility of pure intellectual intuition, except in, or through, the Creator. The true knowledge and the reality of things, or noumenon, is bound to remain unknown and can be apprehended only as an intelligible intuition connected with Being. With a different terminology, one is back to the notion that man knows truth only in God, and as with Spinoza or Augustine, it is only when God creates him or recreates him that man knows that he is truly born. In a different way, in the way which consists in asserting that truth can only be truth as part of the whole, Leibniz and Hegel have said the same thing, and like Leibniz, Bergson maintains that there is, within the whole, a certain individuality of the monad, for though the soul unites with God, it does not entirely merge with God. Bergson's return to psychology as the true field of philosophical studies and metaphysics re-established the contact of the mind with the real, that is to say with the true life or noumenon of things, by apprehending reality from the inside through intuition. This intuition does not apprehend the absolute, or the beatific vision of the mystic, but it does apprehend the duration that is the movement that links with its source which is Being, or with God, for the believer. Bergson is in the line of the great French metaphysicians —Descartes, Pascal and Maine de Biran, and if one excepts the indefinable Rousseau, he is probably the greatest philosopher France has produced since them.

Bergsonism as a theory of knowledge is very close to the theory of aesthetic knowledge, and if one adds to this the fact that

Bergson has written admirably on art, one understands easily why most of the artists of his time found great affinities with, and echoes in his work. Part of his greatness lies in having expressed such a wide span of the sensibility of his time. His brilliance as a lecturer at the Collège de France* attracted not only the mundane, but also great writers and philosophers, from Valéry to T. S. Eliot, Péguy and Jacques Maritain. His philosophical works, written in a fluent and at times poetic style, are, besides their philosophical content, good literature which attracted a wide public.

* The Collège de France, founded by Francis I, is the highest institute of learning in France. It is not part of the University, but has professorial chairs in specialised subjects. There are no students attached to this institute, and no examinations; its lectures are public.

2

Phenomenology

From Kierkegaard to Marx, from Bergson to Edmund Husserl (1859–1938) and Martin Heidegger (b. 1889), thought ceases to concern itself with the world as object, and concerns itself with the world as lived through a subject or *Dasein*. Marx's aim is to transform the world through man, and philosophy is the analysis and ordering of the forces which animate this transforming praxis and which, in the end, should give way to it. Bergson gives pre-eminence to lived duration and lived knowledge over conceptual knowledge; Husserl endeavours to make individual consciousness coincide with the essence of things, and Heidegger tries to wrest the truth about man from *Angst*, the night of nothingness and the openness of Being towards *Dasein*. Husserl and Heidegger are contemporaries of Bergson—Husserl more so than Heidegger. But the important thing is that these two philosophers expounded their philosophical systems and published their main works during Bergson's lifetime. Husserl's *Ideas* was published in 1911, and Heidegger's *Being and Time* in 1927. Whether Bergson knew Husserl's phenomenology or not is irrelevant. What matters is that they both belong to the same age and that they reached similar philosophical conclusions. None of these three philosophers believed that Kant had sounded the death knell of metaphysics, and Heidegger set about explaining that Kant had not meant that metaphysics was impossible, but that it ought to rest on a different basis, and that phenomenology is necessarily ontology. Bergson based his metaphysics on man, psychology and the non-mediated data of consciousness. Heidegger's nothingness is not Sartre's nothingness; it is indistinguishable from the opacity of Being which, through *Angst*, reveals to the existent-*Dasein* some of its veiled or invisible strangeness.

Husserl's phenomenology is, as we shall see, very close to Bergson's philosophy, which is, as has been pointed out, despite its appearances, in some ways seminal to that of Merleau-Ponty and Sartre. For Bergson, to exist is to change, to make or to create oneself indefinitely. Sartre as well as Marx stresses man's capacity to create himself, and this creativeness which is basic to man endows him with the power to become the *logos*, foundation of being, or to play at being God. Phenomenology has been described as the philosophy of creative intuition. Either through the Husserlian notion of the transcendental *I*, or through the Bergsonian duration, man is the being by which the world is partly revealed, in some ways created, known and given meaning. With Claudel, a devout Christian, man rediscovers what is already there, God-given; yet, even the atheistic Valéry thinks that the world thinks itself in man. For Husserl man sees what is there already through a kind of Orphic knowledge of the earth. But the existent can apprehend itself and creation only through connecting with its creative force or Being—that is to say through language, creative *logos*, part of Being. Bergson, Husserl, and Merleau-Ponty are at one on this point.

Husserl's phenomenology, expounded at the beginning of the twentieth century, rapidly assumed a growing importance in Europe, and by the thirties it was already very well-known in France. Husserl believes, like Bergson, that empirical knowledge is purely external and that therefore, setting aside Kantian taboos, one must return to the thing itself. Phenomenology is a method of description of the things themselves and of the world as they appear to the naïve gaze of the onlooker, freed from all conceptual, *a priori* constructions. It is, in fact, a direct intuitive apprehension of the structure or essence of things. The subject who apprehends this inner reality of things is the existent, the *Dasein*, which makes the world appear as it truly is. Phenomenological knowledge is that which encloses itself on its own, as it shows itself on its own; it is a partial revelation of the Being of beings, and that is why phenomenology is ontology. The apprehending subject is an intentional consciousness, and for Husserl as well as for Merleau-Ponty, consciousness is always consciousness of something; it is never a void, a nothingness or an attempt at being a pure consciousness of itself; it is, as it were, a light which illumines things and makes them appear as they truly are. The world is, for and by consciousness, which gives it meaning. Consciousness can apprehend itself in the act of giving meaning to the world, but this act of apprehension is an act of recognition of essence by essence, and not a distancing of a hypothetical *per-se* from a hypothetical *in-se*. Through this act, phenomenology discovers the transcendental structure of consciousness, that is to say the irreducible or transcendental *I* which is the source, or light, of consciousness, and which seems to me to be the individuated essence of Being. A transcendental *I* necessarily implies a plurality of subjects, therefore an intersubjectivity, but avoiding any possible dualism or separation between body and spirit, the transcendental is not separated from the subject it belongs to which is part of history and the world, and this concrete participation in the world is best illustrated by the philosophy of Merleau-Ponty who, in this respect, continues the evolution of Husserl's thought.

According to Husserl, the philosopher aims at reaching a universal knowledge of the world, the total truth about the world as such. But the question to be solved is that which concerns the worth of the experience of a world order, an order of which the subject has an immediate intuitive certainty as a spatio-temporal being, for this certainty is always modified by the changing experience of individual life, and this experience, which is individual, communal and historical, is embedded in a world, part of an ontological necessity continuously open, and, therefore, precluding the possible apprehension of Being in itself. Being—the Absolute—cannot be defined or fully apprehended by something finite—*Dasein*—which is partially knowable. Being can be only apprehended through man, but in itself it always remains wholly other. All knowledge can only be relative, and yet man, a rational being, tends towards generalisation, and universality of knowledge; at least, he does in his philosophical searches, particularly in our age when scientific thought tends to equate knowledge with objectivity. Yet this is for Husserl an impossible dream. 'Attempts have been made to confer upon psychology the same objectivity as pertains to physics, and this has made psychology impossible. In truth, when it comes to the psyche, to subjectivity understood as individual subjectivity, as

an existent in isolation, or as involved in history and in a social
community, it is clearly absurd to confer upon it an objectivity
similar to that of the natural sciences.' (*Being and Thinking*,
French translation by Paul Ricoeur in *Deucalion*, III, éd.
de la Baconnière, Neuchâtel; extract quoted in *Panorama des Idées
Contemporaines*, ed. Gaëtan Picon, Gallimard, 1957, p. 58)
Philosophy, says Husserl, has always been tempted by the objectivity of the natural sciences, and only idealism has tried to deal
with subjectivity as subjectivity, and accepted the fact that the
world is always given to a subject or to a community of subjects,
simply as a world whose value is only relative, subjective, con-
tingent upon an ever changing content of experience, and
therefore always new.

For Husserl, as for Bergson, life is constant becoming, and
personal life unfolds through varying degrees of consciousness
and awareness of personal responsibility. The aim of consciousness is to make for itself a true, free and autonomous self, that
is to say to realise the rationality inherent in it. To remain
faithful to itself as rational being is the aim of the individual
as well as of the community; the individual must realise his
rationality as part of the community, and the community its
own as an aggregate of individuals. 'Philosophy,' says Husserl,
'is only rationalism diversifying itself according to the various
planes on which intention and realisation operate; it is *ratio*
intent upon its ceaseless movement to know itself. . . . Seen from
the inside, philosophy is the ceaseless struggle of "awakened"
reason aspiring to become itself and to reach the knowledge of
its own being and to achieve a rationality which would understand concretely not only itself, but an indubitably existing
world, a world existing in its total and universal truth.' (Quoted
in Gaëtan Picon, *op. cit.*, pp. 60–61) This is somehow Hegelian
thinking. Philosophy for Husserl is as rational as science—a
notion which Sartre describes as that of a madman of genius—
and the task of life is to be rational and to want to be rational.
Reason is that towards which man tends, and reason cannot be
divided, as Kant thought, into theoretical and practical reason,
at least that is what Husserl thinks. And for him, to be a man
is to be teleological, that is to say to be a 'must be'. This
apodictic *telos* can be understood through the understanding of

the self, and to understand it is to understand oneself through *a priori* principles.

The aim of phenomenology is to describe, and not to analyse or explain, and the description aims, by its faithfulness, at recapturing or disclosing the thing itself or essence. It is not without interest to note here that Valéry very often starts one of his poems with a precise phenomenological description of the appearance of an object or a landscape, to rise to an ontological meditation. The aim of phenomenology is to return to the thing itself, to a world in which scientific symbols or abstract definitions have no place. This search for a type of knowledge that Bergson had already outlined coincides with the aim of artistic knowledge, and it is not surprising that Merleau-Ponty was, like Heidegger, more and more interested in art, and that they both succeeded in best expressing some of their views in essays about art. The phenomenological attempt to return to the thing itself is not a return to idealism, though we shall see later that Merleau-Ponty comes quite close to Berkeley.

Descartes' and Kant's knowledge is essentially reflective; the existence of consciousness rests upon the awareness of itself as apprehending a subject which exists through this apprehension. Reflective analysis attempts to unravel the structure or pattern of a thing in order to recapture the inner life of that thing; it is in fact an attempt to retrace, along some kind of Ariadne's thread, the path which, through the labyrinth, leads to the sanctuary where lives the inner flame or force which animates the life or being of the whole. This cannot be done, for there is no Ariadne's thread that could lead from conceptual constructions and reflection to the inner reality of things, because the reflecting *I* merely constructs itself as the goal of its search, while the goal of the search is separated from this self waiting to be disclosed and to be described. Phenomenology starts from the important fact that the world is already out there, before any attempt at apprehension or synthesis is made. That world, for the phenomenologist, is not an object which his inner consciousness unravels, judges or recreates through reflection; it is the field or background of all human thoughts and activities, for man knows himself not in isolation from it, but through it, as an integral part of it and negation of it. This notion is at the root of the famous phenomenological 'reduction'. The world is the representation we have of it, not as men as empirical subjects, but in as far as all men form one single light and are parts of the 'One' without dividing it.

For reflective thought, and for the *cogito* in particular, the *I* can reach itself, and define itself, only by the thought that it has of itself; it is therefore isolated from the other, and Hegel as well as Sartre maintains this isolation of the self. For them, the other is the enemy. For Husserl this is not possible. If the *I* and the other are each one for himself and not both for God or for Being, they are both condemned to have only external views of each other, as one spectator exposed to the gaze of the other, but not as an individual consciousness which could connect with another. The problem for Husserl is therefore to pass from the Cartesian *cogito*, which has been the object of his studies, to a notion of individual consciousness placed in the wider context of human nature and of an historical situation. Then, and then only, is there the possibility of a transcendental subjectivity becoming the intersubjectivity or Being which makes it possible for every individual to feel that he is part and parcel of the world and of creation. In order to become aware of this participation in the world, the individual must withdraw from it and look upon it, as Merleau-Ponty says, 'with amazement', with an unprepared look which reveals its strangeness and its gratuitousness. But as we are part of the world, we can never grasp any more than one aspect of the world, therefore our knowledge of it is always relative, never absolute, always open, never closed, and philosophy for Husserl, as well as for Merleau-Ponty, is a continuous beginning. This openness, this continuous renewal, based on the individual or on the *Dasein*, make of phenomenology the requisite basis of existential thought, for the notion of being in situation or in time, as Heidegger puts it, can only be thought of against a background of phenomenological reduction which presents the world as continuously new to a consciousness in search of its being.

The notion of intentionality, part of Husserl's philosophy, flows from his notion of phenomenological reduction. 'Consciousness,' as he has said, 'is consciousness of something.' Kant, who is never far from Husserl's mind, had made it clear that consciousness, aware of its oneness, anticipates its apprehension of the outside world, and that therefore the unity of the world precedes its knowledge of it, and is lived as something already existing. Nature is discovered as conforming to the laws of the understanding, and imagination conditions the categorical configurations upon which rests the oneness of consciousness. Husserl distinguishes between voluntary intentionality and operating intentionality which is not formulated, and which provides the background which underlies our knowledge. Within this kind of distinction, to understand is not only to know conceptually the properties and various generic intentions of the thing perceived, but to discover its structure, the way and the why it lives. This is nothing less than the Platonic or Hegelian 'idea' which determines, in every way, the life of any given thing in the world; it is the force or essence that makes it live and causes all the manifestations of its being. There are no accidents, there is no hazard in history; everything connects in order to fit within the human situation, which, in truth, must always be examined as a whole, and not from one single standpoint; and all things must be placed within the context of existence. The existent or *Dasein* cannot have a free choice as to whether or not it comes into existence, and truth is only in so far and as long as *Dasein* is, and *Dasein's* mode of being is to be concerned with the truth of its being, so that the relationship between the one and the whole is understandable. There is a meaning in everything, and there are no accidents in existence. They are all subsumed in reason; as Merleau-Ponty put it : 'Because we are in the world, we are condemned to meaning, and we cannot do or say anything which does not take a name in history.'

The phenomenal is not pure being, but the meaning that emerges from the encounter of a subjective experience with it, and with that of other subjects, so as to form an all-embracing intersubjectivity. The *I* does not link up with an existing rationality; it makes one through its own initiative. Phenomenology does not aim at analysing an already existing thing, but at founding or basing being on truth, for truth is an essential mode of being of the existent; but this criterion of what truth is, is difficult to establish, since there is no pre-existing reason or *logos*, and since one starts, not from a possible, but from a real world which the existent constantly endeavours to apprehend and to complete.

Phenomenology as revelation of the world rests upon itself, and founds itself, says Husserl. This is obviously a somewhat abstract and evasive statement which, translated into concrete terms, hypostatises the knowing subject knowing himself through communication with the world, as knowledge of the world. Husserl, like Bergson, sees philosophy as an infinite meditation, continuously open, the task of which is to reveal the mystery of the world and the mystery of reason; its aims are, therefore, cognate with those of art; they meet with Valéry's ceaseless attempts to capture the very dawning of consciousness, with Proust's explorations of the emergence of memory and with Cézanne's searches for the perennial in the life of men and of creation.

3

Maurice Merleau-Ponty

Merleau-Ponty (1908–61) succeeded Bergson at the Collège de France, and his philosophy is more closely connected with that of his predecessor than is acknowledged by many studies of his work. His name is of course associated with that of Husserl, as his best interpreter and follower, and with that of his schoolmate and contemporary, Jean-Paul Sartre, with whom he was, for a time, co-editor of *Les Temps Modernes.* The latter relationship was an uneasy friendship, with ups and downs, and misunderstandings which mutual respect might have cleared away had certain reticences and basic differences of temperament been overcome, and had Merleau-Ponty lived longer. Sartre has admirably and tactfully described the pattern of this friendship in a long essay devoted to Merleau-Ponty and published in *Situations V*. In it, he shows that these two unhappy twins of philosophy were somehow beset by some kind of Greek fate which made it impossible for them to live for long in perfect harmony. The conspectus of their work makes clear at one glance the reason why they could not travel for long side by side. Merleau-Ponty moves from one point to another at a steady pace, though with some pauses and slight diversions on the way. Sartre, on the other hand, is all over the place, and can meet and travel with Merleau-Ponty only when their respective roads intersect and when they go for a brief spell in exactly the same direction.

The graph of Merleau-Ponty's journey, though not easy to assess, is certainly easy to plot. He moved steadily and naturally from phenomenology to ontology, with a few brief halts on the way for the careful examination of artistic and linguistic problems, and the topical political questions in which he was deeply interested, though, of course, never to the same extent as Sartre. Merleau-Ponty was single-minded in his pursuit of true knowledge, haunted by regret for a lost guiding light, finally discovering not so much a guiding light as a ground for the certainty and reality of existence.

Sartre, who is, with Picasso, the most versatile and influential genius of his age, leaves no stone unturned in pursuit of the kind of truth to which he is attracted. Philosopher, dramatist, novelist, psychologist, essayist, political writer, he has achieved, in each of these disciplines, enough success and enough of a reputation to satisfy a more than average talent, and certainty to call for rewards, such as the Nobel Prize, election to the Academy and other honours, which his uncompromising moral integrity forbids him to accept. Merleau-Ponty's moral integrity has certainly nothing in which to envy Sartre's, and it seems to me that his contribution to philosophy, though much less known, because it has not benefited, like that of Sartre, from a wide-ranging popularisation through plays and novels, is more coherent, more rigorously philosophic than Sartre's which, up to a point, suffers from his constant preoccupation with politics and, above all, with psychology, of which he is admittedly a master.

From *La Structure du Comportement*, Merleau-Ponty's first book published in 1942, to *Le Visible et l'Invisible*, published posthumously in 1963, there has been a considerable, though very natural, evolution in his philosophy. The graph of his development, leaving aside politics which did not seem to weigh constantly on his mind, is not unlike that of his master Husserl. *La Phénoménologie de la Perception*, which was his doctoral thesis, and which he published in 1945, is his central work. For Merleau-Ponty perception is the basis of man's reflections, and the body, anchored in the world, part of the world, is the basis of perception. Sartre reproaches him with forgetting history, but Merleau-Ponty, who is more systematic than Sartre, came to history through politics. What he cannot accept is the Sartrian cleavage between the *I* and the other, and between what Sartre calls the *in-se* and the *per-se*. These divisions are for Merleau-Ponty—and I agree with him—artificial and unreal; their elements are, on the contrary, part of a whole, visible or invisible, conscious or pre-conscious, which cannot be conceptualised, and which can be only partially known as subjectivity, bathed in opacity and ambiguity. Non-thought, for him, is inherent in thought, and the *cogito* starts from non-reflection, or pre-reflection. Evidently both non-thought and pre-reflection are indefinable and unknowable, but it is obvious that Merleau-Ponty wants to avoid the Cartesian equation of *cogito* with Being, and he wants to maintain the reality of Being as under-lying thought and the importance of unconceptualised perception as the means of seeing and knowing the world. 'True philosophi-cal knowledge,' he says in *Eloge de la Philosophie*, 'is perception.' (Gallimard, 1953, p. 25)

La Phénoménologie de la Perception is first and foremost an amazed return to the simple elements and to the difficulty of grasping non-mediated appearances which contain the secret of their being. This secret can be grasped only through the naïve direct perception of the phenomenal appearance or disclosure. 'The first philosophical act would be to reach the living world which precedes the objective world, and to rediscover the phenomenon, to reawaken perception and to unmask the dis-guise by which it makes it possible for itself to be forgotten as a fact and as a perception.' (*La Phénoménologie de la Percep-tion*, Gallimard, p. 69) But this non-mediated perception is extremely difficult to apprehend, for it is extremely difficult to reach the non-objective, pre-reflective world without involving reflection and all that goes with it, that is to say thinking about thought; yet, says Merleau-Ponty, 'if to reflect is to try to redis-cover the origins, that by which being and thinking are possible, reflection cannot confine itself to objective thought, it must think exactly the acts and the thematisations of objective thought and reconstruct its context.' (*Ibid.*, p. 334) The pre-reflective world must not be equated with the subconscious, for it is something more opaque and more all-embracing than the psychoanalytical notion of the subconscious; it is a kind of uncharted, unfathomed, transcendental field which underlies the whole life of mankind, and out of which individual subjectivity carves and constructs its relationship with others and with the world. This relationship rests, not upon any Sartrian notion of a reflecting subject assert-ing its existence and project against the viscosity or *in-se* of the world, but upon a subjective non-reflective activity seeking to establish its true relationship with the world. 'It is not the *I think* which pre-eminently contains the *I am*, it is not my existence which is reduced to the consciousness I have of it; it is, on the contrary, the *I think* which is reintegrated into the movement of transcendence of the *I am*, and consciousness into existence.' (*Ibid.*, p. 439) The aim is to recapture the genesis of existence, and that cannot be done through the intellect, but only through the body which is the basis of perception.

To perceive is to be involved with things, and that before there is any conscious awareness of the existence of these things. The body behaves as a subject, centre of perceptions, perceiving and being perceived, a creative structure developing in time according to its own individual duration, connecting directly or intuitively in a Bergsonian fashion with the truth of things, and being, therefore, part of the harmony or synthesis which underlies human temporality. The body is a complex of living meanings, bent on its own equilibrium, and capable of pre-conceptual self-knowledge, which emerges probably at the point where one passes from primal instinct to intuition. For Merleau-Ponty, the body is a structure open to the world, correlative with the world, it is in the world, it is our anchor in and our mediator with the world. 'Things and the world are given to me with the parts of my body, in a living connection, comparable or rather identical with that which exists between the various parts of my own body.' (*Ibid.*, p. 239) There is therefore a continuous interpenetration between the body and the world, both bathing in the same substratum of laws and substances which unites them, so that before any form of conceptualisation and reflective apprehension of the world takes place, the world is already there, felt, perceived and recorded by the human body. The being in the world or *Dasein* always precedes the reflective consciousness of the world, which it organises and transforms, according to its own established conceptual structures. The aim of phenomenology is, as Merleau-Ponty, quoting Husserl, put it, the direct apprehension of reality : 'it is pure and, one might say, non-formalised experience which must be made to achieve the pure expression of its own meaning.' (*Ibid.*, p. 254) It is easy to see how close the aim of phenomenology is to Bergson's search for duration.

According to Merleau-Ponty we are haunted by the primal world from which we have emerged, and our contacts with the world are therefore pre-conscious, pre-scientific, pre-objective; they are a direct perceptive awareness of our relationship with it. 'We know nothing yet of the world and of objective space, we try to describe the phenomena of the world, that is to say its forces in the field in which perception places us when we are still alone, when the others appear only later, and when knowledge and, in particular, science have not yet reduced and levelled individual perspective.' (*Ibid.*, p. 296) Perception lies therefore at the root of scientific knowledge and thinking, and 'thought is not detachable from language. . . . There is no pure thought, the thinking subject rests upon an existent subject.' (*Ibid.*, p. 225) Ideas and things emerge from a kind of primal world; the world is in fact 'an immense individual'; it could be the great One of Blake, or possibly the *anima mundi* of Yeats or Jung; it is, anyway, an open totality, an inexhaustible reserve of temporality inhabited by coexisting individuals, tied to it by their bodies by virtue of the original contract of birth in the world. A kind of essential force which informs time or existence moves through the primal world, flows forth, and results in a kind of endless creation of beings or subjectivities. 'We are the emergence of time.' (*Ibid.*, p. 485) We rejoin the Kantian notion of time making itself through man. 'The world is inseparable from the subject, but from a subject which is nothing but project of the world, and the subject is inseparable from the world, but from a world which it projects.' (*Ibid.*, p. 491) The subject, the *I*, constructs the reality of the world through language, and the relationship of the *I* to the world is a continuously altering synthesis moving towards its finality which is to know itself as an assertion of the existence of an ontological reality or Being.

Merleau-Ponty who, like Husserl, goes over and over again the problems raised by the Cartesian *cogito*, makes clear his phenomenological and existential views that the *cogito* is only *cogito* once it has been expressed, through a subject, and that this subject as a body is in the world as project of the world, thinks as a being in the world, and is himself by being to the world. The world is open and yet one, and subjectivity is also both open and one, part of a universal intersubjectivity or Being, from which existence or temporality emerges, so that there is complete coincidence between existence, subjectivity, and the body which unites both with the world.

After *La Phénoménologie de la Perception*, Merleau-Ponty turned his attention to the everyday activities of the world. He had, during the war, taken part in the Resistance, and in 1947 he published *Humanisme et Terreur*, which shows political beliefs and attitudes far more radical than those of Sartre, even though, in the end, he proved to be much less attracted by Marxism than Sartre. He could never admit that historical materialism could possibly be the only guiding force in history, impervious to alterations and changes. Merleau-Ponty's thought was flexible, always open to new possibilities, ever unwilling to fall into any rigid pattern. In this respect, he was not unlike Montaigne; he looked upon historical events and enterprises as adventures, without any fixed structure of development, and he felt that Marxism did not make enough allowance for contingencies. So he accepted it as a regulating, guiding idea and as a heuristic science which corresponded to his humanitarianism, but he deplored its excesses, and in fact he parted company with Sartre on account of them. He had reached the conclusion, admirably analysed and described in his studies of Marxism, that after the Industrial Revolution the proletariat had become unable to carry alone the torch of revolution, for the proletariat had evolved and was no longer the alienated class that is the perfect antithesis of capitalism.

Merleau-Ponty does not seem to have ever completely forgotten his Christian upbringing and his vague longing for an absent transcendence and metaphysics to which, like Husserl and Heidegger, he returned in his later writings, published posthumously. The period in between is occupied by his co-editorship of *Les Temps Modernes* with Sartre, his teaching at the Collège de France, from 1952 onwards, and the writing of a brilliant collection of essays on art, politics and philosophy which came out in book form under the titles of *Eloge de la Philosophie*, *Signes, Sens et Non-sens*, and *Les Aventures de la Dialectique* in which he outlined his distance from Sartre's 'bolshevism'. In 1953 he lost his mother, to whom he was deeply attached; he was profoundly upset, and refused to believe in a complete and final separation. He could not accept the title of Christian any more than that of atheist; he chose to keep himself, as always, open to searches and to discoveries which took him beyond phenomenology, in pursuit of the relationship between the existent and Being.

In order to think, one has to be, and to be is not to be in isolation, but to belong to Being—to be both individuated from it and part of it—and to be from birth condemned to death and to know it, therefore to try, throughout the stretch of time between, to delay it or to survive it, while still not being sure of rejoining the absolute. That is the problem for man, and the only way to attempt to solve it, for the atheist, is through art, through language expressing man's *logos*; the notion of *logos* is of course ambiguous, and it goes well beyond the limitations of atheism. Merleau-Ponty was aware of this, and his non-dogmatic attitude enabled him to follow the explorations suggested by a form of thinking that found it impossible to isolate past, present and future in separate compartments. He believed that man's task is to unify, through his vision, attuned to the deep structures of nature, the various phenomenal aspects of nature and to reduce multiplicity to oneness.

Whether Merleau-Ponty's thought was influenced by events in his life such as the death of his mother, and by the growing importance of Heidegger's thought, or whether it was purely a normal development or growth of his own, perfectly paralleled by the graph of his later master Heidegger, is difficult to decide. The fact is that, through his years of meditation between *La Phénoménologie de la Perception* and the elaboration of his thought only partially achieved in *Le Visible et l'Invisible*, he had been deeply concerned with language and with the logical development of phenomenology towards ontology. Some of his studies of language were published in *Sens et Non-sens*, and the others were issued in 1969 under the title of *La Prose du Monde*. With *La Phénoménologie de la Perception*, Merleau-Ponty had perfected an excellent instrument for assessing the true nature of perceptions and their relations with the nature of being as *logos*, expressed by the *logos* or being of language. This had led him to the threshold of new openings which he would have had to face, or take a new direction. He left, alas, his task unfinished, because he was interrupted by death, practically in the middle of his speech, yet what he left behind him makes quite clear what he was aiming at and where he was going. In *La Phénoménologie de la Perception* he had stated that Descartes' *cogito* presupposes a pre-reflective contact of oneself with oneself as tacit *cogito*. In *Le Visible et l'Invisible* he says: 'What I call the tacit *cogito* is impossible. In order to be aware of the idea of "thinking" . . . , to perform the "reduction", to return to immanence and to the consciousness of . . . it is necessary to have words.' (Pp. 224–25) Words are necessary to construct this transcendental consciousness which does not correspond to something already existing, but on the contrary emerges from the ambient creative silence. Thus the philosopher, like the artist, moves from a state of semi-obscurity and unknowingness to light and knowledge, and silence is not the opposite of speech, but the surrounding and therefore the setting-off element or climate of speech, which surges from, and returns to, silence.

There is a being of language that repeats the being of Being, and to think is to pass from the source of being to speech or existence. Man, as Heidegger put it, *is* only in so far as he is 'saying' (or speaking), disclosing the essence of Being. Man is man in so far as he is devoted to the call of language; he is used for language. The end of *Le Visible et l'Invisible* sums up Merleau-Ponty's philosophical aim: 'In one sense, as Husserl says, the whole of philosophy consists in recreating a power of signifying, a dawning of meaning, or an uncharted meaning, an expression of experience through experience which illuminates the special domain of language. And in a sense, as Valéry says, language is all, since it is nobody's voice; it is the true voice of things, waters and woods. What must be understood is that these two views are not dialectically opposed, and we do not have to reassemble them into a synthesis: they are two aspects of reversibility, which is the ultimate truth.' (Pp. 203–04) There is no frontier between language and the world, silence goes on beyond speech, for it is clear that both are part of the same substratum of being. Merleau-Ponty's views on language as the instrument of philosophic explorations show that far from dreaming of confining philosophy's task to explorations of language, he sees philosophy as an unveiling of meanings, and this unveiling concerns Being.

The philosophical possibilities of exploring the range of Being are best met if one uses language as creativity, as it is used in art, as it was used, at times, by Plato. In this way, its range of meaning and illumination, its creative force, is never confined to the present as it is in the case of language used as a pure and simple means of communication; it remains, on the contrary, always open, as a basis of ever-renewed, ever-changing durations. 'The words most laden with philosophy are not necessarily those which enclose what they say. They are those which open most energetically upon being, because they convey more exactly the life of the whole and disturb, to breaking point, our well established certainties. The question is whether philosophy as a rediscovery of unfathomed being can best be served by means of logical language or by using language not as a means of conveying direct, immediate meaning but as an equivalent of what it would like to say.' (*Ibid.*, p. 358) This means that in such cases, where exact conveyance of meaning cannot be reached, language should be used not as a means of communication but as a creative instrument, in the way the poet uses it in order to organise it into a poem which is an entity endlessly alive, and which suggests or attempts to convey the logically inexpressible. We are well away from Wittgenstein's thought: 'What we cannot speak about we pass over in silence', right into the Mallarméan world in which language can suggest musically the presence of something that is not there.* We are also well away from the notion of silence as an opposite of speech, and right into the notion which looks upon language and silence as being as closely connected as shadow and light. 'Speech is an integral part of meanings as the flesh of the visible, connected with Being through a being and, like flesh, narcissistic, eroticised, endowed with the natural capacity to attract into its net other meanings as the body perceives the world in perceiving itself.' (*Ibid.*, p. 158) Then follows the very Hegelian thought: 'Life becomes

---

* 'Je dis: une fleur, et hors de l'oubli où ma voix relègue aucun contour, en tant que quelque chose d'autre que les calices sus, musicalement se lève, idée même et suave, l'absente de tous bouquets.' S. Mallarmé, *Oeuvres Complètes*, Gallimard, Paris, 1945, p. 368.

ideas, and the ideas return to life, everyone is caught in the whirlpool in which at first he committed only moderate stakes, led on by what he has said and the reply that was given him, and by his thought which is no longer the outcome of his isolated thinking.' (*Ibid.*, p. 159) This admirable grasp of the relationship of ideas to life and vice-versa, and of the organicity of the thinking *I*, leads to the acceptance of a relationship between individuated experience and Being as something which defies conceptual analysis and examination. 'Ideas are the texture of experience, its style, unexpressed at first, then expressed. Like every style they at first ripen in the heart of Being, and they cannot, on any grounds, be detached from it to be laid out before an inspecting gaze.' (*Ibid.*, pp. 159–60) The ideas have therefore ontological connotations, and they are the substratum of language which is the means of corresponding with and responding to Being.

In *La Phénoménologie de la Perception*, Merleau-Ponty had ignored the structure of the awareness of the world of intentionality and the ontological connotations of these operations. In *Le Visible et l'Invisible* he tries to deal with these problems and to scrutinise and understand the moment at which the subject becomes both part of the world and visible to the world. The body is indeed a two-dimensional fragment of being; it is, on one side, a perceiving mass, and, on the other, a seen mass; it is both looking and being looked at, reflecting and being reflected upon, and this complex structure is truly the archetypal structure of being. 'Because perception gives us faith in a world and in a system of natural, rigorously connected and continuous facts, we believed that this system could incorporate everything, including the perception which initiated us into it. Today, we no longer believe such things . . . and our task is to understand in what way and in what sense what is not nature forms a "world", what is a "world", and lastly, if world there is, what is the relationship between the visible and the invisible world.' (*Ibid.*, pp. 46–47) Merleau-Ponty had by now come to the conclusion that phenomenology was not enough, that philosophy cannot content itself with describing the world and, least of all, with attempts to equate itself with science and scientific methods.

Science, according to Merleau-Ponty, can only survey its

object from above, and it generally tends to equate knowledge and being. Like Bergson, he believes that scientific knowledge is analytical, conceptual and turns everything it deals with into objects, while philosophy is something different; it does not deal with the world as object; it asks questions about the world, and these questions always involve the subject who asks them. The questioner questions himself, and whatever reality he discovers is always grounded in the reality of his own self which is more mysterious and more fundamental than any aspect of the world that the philosopher seeks to understand. Reflective philosophy replaces the world by the thought of being, conceives the thinking subject as thought, and thus renders impossible any relation with other thinking subjects. We are thus in a closed world of mental monadism, watched over by a distant God—the world of Descartes. Through reflection, the thinking *I*, lost in his perceptions, rediscovers himself in rediscovering them as mental states, thinks that he thinks and, therefore, always operates on the plane of idealisation and after-the-event, and never on the primary plane of creating or making the event. This is the price one has to pay if one confines perception to its mental representation, for, by so doing, one ignores all the possibilities of nonexistence that are inherent in it; one equates the negation of negation and our relationship with being with the discursive operation by which we repel illusions as well as the possible or the probable.

'Each perception,' says Merleau-Ponty, 'carries the possibility of its replacement by another, . . . it is the end of a continuity, of a series of "illusions" which were not only simple "thoughts" . . . but possibilities which could have been . . . and which, as such, never return to nothingness or to subjectivity, but rather, as Husserl puts it, are "rubbed out" or "scored out" by the "new" reality.' (*Ibid.*, p. 65) A perception carries with it both the visible and the invisible, which should not be ignored, as it is ignored by reflective thought. Husserl's and Merleau-Ponty's aim is to grasp the inner reality of things, and transcendental reduction implies the subject's detachment from the affective unfolding of his perceptions and of his perception of the world, and his concentration on seizing their essence, their direction or their disclosure of the true reality of the world. This world pre-exists our perception of it, and is the same for all; it is always beyond our thoughts, and our varied perceptions of it leave it unchanged, yet carrying around it an aura of spiritual or permanent oneness to which we, at times, accede, through our relationship with others and with the world as voice or representation of Being, and through intersubjectivity, by recognising, as Hegel, quoted by Merleau-Ponty, put it, that 'to turn into oneself is to get out of oneself' (*ibid.*, p. 74), or by following Heidegger's advice to look upon *Dasein* as the servant of Being and on language as its true voice.

The true self is also the transcendental self, the intersubjective to which all selves have access; the invisible, the unthought, the implicit, the unrealised, the possible and probable, all these are forms of negation which underlie Being. Therefore the intuition of Being is always simultaneous with the intuition of the negation of nothingness. Nothingness is what is not, it has no attributes or predicates. 'There is only Being,' says Merleau-Ponty. '. . . If nothingness is destined to Being, my presence as nothingness is a project for totality and cohesion which postulates that it is the same being that is in question. . . . Everything that is fragmentary is destined to be reintegrated, every negation is in reality individuation, and being oneself, being the other and being *in-se* are fragments of one single Being; negativism, if it is rigorous and absolute, is a kind of positivism.' (*Ibid.*, pp. 91–92) There is not something rather than nothing, for nothing could never take the place of something or of being. Nothingness does not exist, while being is, and the exact coincidence of the one with the other leaves no room for questions. Negation must be thought of as negation of nothingness, that is to say as part of an activity and not as an entity. Nothingness cannot be incorporated in Being because it has no being, and it is therefore indistinguishable from Being; it is because nothingness is absolutely non-existent that it can only be conceived of as a shadowy area of non-being, floating around the real world of Being. Nothingness is neither an alternative to, nor an ingredient of, Being, but it is implied in the negating capability of Being which is negation of negation, negation of all virtualities and possibilities that are attracted towards being or existence, and therefore could be, and yet, lacking sufficient being, remain as the invisible shadow of the visible. Therefore this negation of negation is a moment that contributes to the making and self-knowing of Being, and as such is undetachable from Being. The *in-se* and *per-se* of Sartre dissolve themselves into Being which is, and nothingness which is not. Sartre's idea of nothingness is a pseudo-idea, for the truth of the Latin tag : *ex nihilo nihil* seems to me incontrovertible.

Merleau-Ponty has a very different notion of Being. 'Being will be that without which there would be neither a world, nor language, nothing whatever; it will be essence.' (*Ibid.*, p. 145) Here the key word that clearly separates Merleau-Ponty's existentialism from that of Sartre is explicitly used, and it is the word 'essence'. This notion of essence will be examined later when I deal with existentialism; for the moment, what matters is the exact philosophical position of Merleau-Ponty. Two pages later he makes it crystal clear by placing himself with the essentialists in philosophy and with the teleological evolutionists in biology. 'Without the necessities of essence, their unbreakable connections, their irresistible implications, resistant and stable structures, there would be neither world, nor anything in general, nor Being.' (*Ibid.*, p. 147) Merleau-Ponty makes it clear that this essence does not yield the primordial meaning of Being, nor can it be looked upon as the cause of being or of the world. Individuated essence can only connect with Being if it emerges into the living experience of a *Dasein*, surrounded by living experiences, by the present world and by existent beings, whose essence or *ex-sistence* is the standing out into the truth of Being and the revelation of Being.

There are no essences without the notion of space or time; they are part and parcel of the experience of the world, lived through individuated consciousnesses which connect with one another as part of the same ontological revelation of Being. There are worlds, there is a world and there is Being, not a total of facts or system of ideas, but an impossibility of non-sense or ontological void. Space and time are not a sum of individuals temporal and localised. There is on the contrary an underlying latency behind each and all of these aspects of life. The questions 'Where am I?' and 'What time is it?' lie unseparated above facts, and below the 'essences', in unfathomed Being, behind the barrier of our acquired knowledge. To be hidden is one of the qualities of Being, therefore its discovery can never be achieved or can only be something incomplete and fragmentary. The moment the individual has an awareness of Being, he himself ceases to be aware of himself, therefore the awareness of Being is always the consciousness of the past. Bergson, quoted by Merleau-Ponty, said, 'our intuition is reflection . . . the secret of Being is enclosed in an integrity or oneness which is behind us.' (*Ibid.*, p. 165)

The problem is to discover the truth or essence of things, 'to find a language that could enable things to speak, a language that would not be organised by the philosopher, who would allow the words to organise themselves through him, according to the natural interplay of their meaning, through the occult action of the metaphor, what matters being not the evident meaning of each word and each image, but the cognate relationships and connections which are implied in their movement and exchanges. This is the kind of language that Bergson claimed for philosophers.' (*Ibid.*, p. 167) This is also the dream of the later Heidegger who looks upon language as the voice of Being expressing man through the Holy Spirit. This is also the language of poetry, the language of the imagination, which does not describe and define, but which unveils the truth or being of things. Man himself is inside Being, endowed with being, therefore we cannot pretend not to be, or not to know that we are, for these assertions or experiences remain part of Being.

Being cannot be approached through assessments or measurements of time or the relationships between its component elements. 'Being can reveal itself, as Bergson put it [in *La Pensée et le Mouvant*], only to those whose sole aim is to see it, and who, because they have not planned to seize it, connect through vision with its internal movement.' (*Ibid.*, p. 170) Merleau-Ponty, like Heidegger, moved more and more towards the philosophy which has been the most seminal of the age, that of Bergson. 'Being,' he said, 'is what requires form in creation so that we may experience it.' (*Ibid.*, p. 251) Heidegger, not influenced by Bergson, devoted the same concern as Bergson to proving that in spite of Kant or, as he says, with Kant's implicit approval, metaphysics is still possible. Like Bergson he is deeply interested in the arts, and his studies of the poet Hölderlin represent the most penetrating approach ever achieved to this difficult and admirable poet. Merleau-Ponty displayed the same passionate interest in the arts and suggested that philosophy could be envisaged as art. His views on language as a complex entity transcending historical time, his sense of the concrete, of the importance of the body as the basis of the visible and the seen, connecting all, bring philosophy closer to art (thus fulfilling Nietzsche's dream), and to the idea that the world is one. In this case, if we do not quite have the Baudelairean correspondences, we do have certain correspondences between the awareness of the presence of other beings and the innate consciousness which we have of this awareness.

Literature, music and painting are looked upon as the unveiling of truths which are part of, or wrapped in physical reality, and which can be experienced only through the senses. They are and must always remain hallowed by darkness, and they are the proof that the great night of the soul is not empty and is not nothingness, that absence is not total non-existence, and that therefore, beyond sound, light or coherences in words, there are elements waiting for emergence into visibility, sound and meaning. The body is neither idea nor thing, it is both, being the measure of things that surround it. Ideas are not nothingness; it is the invisible which underlies the world that renders it visible, for it is the being of what is. We are practically in the midst of Christian orthodoxy, in the world of the *ens* as the subsistent force and cause of the life of the world, or in the world of Heidegger in which man—*Dasein*—is necessary to the self-disclosure of the truth or essence of Being, and is projected by Being into *ex-sistence* as its self-disclosure and revelation of truth. 'If one explained completely the architectonics of the human body, its ontological structure and the way it sees and hears itself, one would see that the structure of its silent world is such that all the possibilities of speech are already contained in it.' (Merleau-Ponty, *ibid.*, p. 203)

There is no dualism in Merleau-Ponty's philosophy. Body and soul are conceived of as two aspects of one single, sensible, visible world which is connected with Being which is the source of all things. What is called the soul or essence is not implanted in the body, it is an inherent part of it as projection of Being, as speech is to man the saying of essence, so that the beginning of speech is not truly a beginning, but merely the returning of an absence, or the emergence of a hidden presence which is Being. 'Spirit emerges like water in the gap of Being. There is no need to look for spiritual things, there are only structures in the void. I simply wish to plant this void in the visible Being and show that it is its obverse, and in particular the obverse of language.' (*Ibid.*, p. 289) 'Negative and positive mean nothing to me, they are synonymous . . . I take my point of departure at the point where Sartre finishes, the point where Being is taken back by the for-itself. It is for him a point of arrival because he starts from being and negativity and he constructs their union. For me, it is structure or transcendence which explains, and being and nothingness (in Sartre's meaning) are two abstract properties of it. An internal ontology does not require the building up of transcendence; this transcendence is, first and foremost, like Being, lined with nothingness, and what has to be explained is the separation of the one from the other (something never achieved). . . . To describe structure, that is the problem.' (*Ibid.*, p. 290) Here is a clear-cut difference from Sartre who lays constant stress on the importance of the self, and ignores or decries the importance of Being as the substratum of existence. For Merleau-Ponty, whatever happens in the world is possible because there is being, not being in itself, identical with itself, therefore closed, but being which contains its negativity, its capacity to perceive and to be perceived, so that *ex-sistence* and beings are the means through which consciousness emerges as revelation of being, and being corresponds, in fact, to modes of the structuring of consciousness as means of the self-disclosure of Being.

Merleau-Ponty's philosophy is a philosophy of oneness. Being is, and becomes one through the existent who is through Being, but this always implies the existence of others or of the other, and the confirmation of Husserl's notion that transcendental consciousness is intersubjectivity. One cannot see without being at the same time visible. The body is caught up in the structure of the world, and the world is made of the same stuff as the body, therefore there is a constant interpenetration between the one

and the other, and the structures of Being which the mind perceives in nature are inevitably analogous to, or similar to, the
structures of the mind of the observing subject. What we see,
what we know, is always a form of self-seeing and self-knowing,
because one could not see or recognise something which has no
structural correspondences with our vision or with the structures
of our consciousness which links us with Being. There is and
there is bound to be unity and similarity of coding, or of basic
structure between the individuated being and other manifestations of Being, either as other beings, or as parts of the
phenomenal world, and there must therefore be levels of meaning at which individuation ceases, so as to become one meaning,
one kind of ecstasy, reflected through variously individuated
subjectivities, connected to the same source, yet knowing each its
own individuality as living in the same milieu, within the enfolding oneness of Being.

The artist's function is to go beyond the unformulated truth
of Being and to express or to reveal Being, to make it apprehensible to the senses and to the imagination. This is the task not
only of the artist but also of man, of history and of philosophy,
and it is undeniably Merleau-Ponty's task in the latter part of
his life. Like Bergson, he reached the conclusion that absence is
richer in meaning than presence, and also that the being of the
dead is part of the being of the living, united in a kind of
indivisible communion which links existence with Being, and
which, therefore, unavoidably leads phenomenology towards
ontology. This move took place without any shift of the primacy
of man to that of Being or of the Absolute, as is the case with
the later Heidegger. Yet, without positing the primacy of Being,
Merleau-Ponty looks upon man as destined to exteriorise and
to realise and disclose Being, and as therefore endowed with a
teleology that carries with it the structures of Being and is
destined to express it. Without accepting transcendence, Merleau-
Ponty returns to a form of Hegelian immanentism that we find
in Bergson's as well as in Teilhard de Chardin's thought. This
type of immanentism is of the very texture of late nineteenth-
and early twentieth-century art, an immanentism that hypostatises art as Being.

The artist's task, whether he be Mallarmé or Rilke, is to

make Being or the invisible partly visible; for Mallarmé the poetic act, the poem, was all that there was to be seen or experienced; before it, there was nothing; beyond it, nothing. Art is a shooting star going from nowhere to nowhere, abolishing for a few brief seconds the dark, silent skies. But Mallarmé was exceptional, and none but he was so obsessed with the reduction of the absolute to the flickering light of the human brain, or of the human consciousness. Painters, from those of the caves of Lascaux to Rembrandt, Cézanne and Picasso, have always been, in their various ways, concerned with the task of making Being visible, and whether they call this Being God, the primeval force which sends the sap through the green world, the teleological finality which leads Being to reveal and to know itself, or the biological creativity which guides creation to greater and greater complexity and higher degrees of consciousness, this purposefulness can manifest itself only through man who is the only one in nature who makes knowledge of this metaphysical travail possible.

Merleau-Ponty's philosophy is a philosophy of reconciliation between certain apparently conflicting points of view, a reconciliation permeated by the conflicting ideas of his time. He tried to reveal the individual man, rooted in nature to which he belongs, and part and parcel of history which he makes, through which he knows himself, and which thus passes from the singular to the universal and becomes valid for all men. We can see here why Merleau-Ponty, though never a Marxist, was always very close to Marxism, particularly to the Marxist view of history, a view that is above all existential. For Merleau-Ponty, Being can only show itself or emerge through men, and this apprehension of Being is not remote from the Bergsonian or Heideggerian type of illumination obtained by saints and mystics which keeps mankind's vision always open to new horizons never reached but lying beyond the bounds of habits and conceptual knowledge. These moments of illumination are moments of incarnation, of Being made flesh; they are also Hegelian moments where what matters is not so much Being, whose essence is unfathomable, as its incarnation, its immanent power to transform life into essence or into its ashes which transcend time. To do so, the absolute becomes what Merleau-Ponty would call the invisible, and the other side or obverse of this invisible becomes the body, and the body is what truly matters, for, as the centre of consciousness and the senses, the body suffers, feels and also assesses, through itself, the infinite variety and perenniality of the world.

In fact, the great problem for man is not to risk impossible generalisations, plunge into Cartesian assertions, or offer solutions that reason does not warrant and that man's conscience can countenance only by passing from reverence for perceptions and rationality to dreams and fantasies, but to remain open to, and to be always aware of all men, individually and all together, aware that each one of them is making his own contribution to an ever moving light which illumines the heart-breaking yet steady progress of mankind, something that Merleau-Ponty has admirably described in a text called *L'Oeil et l'Esprit*. This is, in many ways, his philosophical testament and I quote a passage from it which sums up his very humane and ever open philosophy: 'If we cannot establish a hierarchy of civilisations or talk of progress, through the history of painting or other arts, it is not because we are held back by some kind of destiny, but rather because, in a certain sense, the first paintings went straight to the depth of the future. If no painting can put an end to painting, no creative work is absolutely finished; each creation changes, alters, illumines, deepens, confirms, exalts, re-creates or creates all the others in advance. If artistic creations are not an end in themselves, it is not only because, like all things, they pass; it is also because they have the greater part of their lives in front of them.' (*L'Oeil et l'Esprit*, Gallimard, 1964, pp. 92–93)

Merleau-Ponty answers Sartre's assertion that we are condemned to be free with the assertion that we are condemned to meaning. To Marxist pseudo-objectivism and Sartrian subjectivism he opposes the view that history is made by beings whose consciousness is not dissolved into the whole but is, on the contrary, incarnated in and mediated by realities and social structures. History is neither meaningless nor determined, it has a meaning which rests upon the human being as a concrete entity aware of his transience and solidarity with other human beings.

4

Existentialism

The human mind, attuned to nature, part of nature, possesses in itself the structures that are part of the laws of nature, and therefore slowly and progressively throughout the unfolding of mankind's life, discovers them or re-cognises them. Man cannot read the great book of nature at one single glance; for that, he would have to be God, and he would not therefore be part of individuated existence or being, and being, as previously noted, is the means and the necessity by which essence has to be and to know itself. Man, as existent, moves towards the Absolute or God, and co-operates with Him in the reading and making of the great book of nature, and reason—*logos*—discovers and, through its discoveries, reveals the exact state of human society at the time when these discoveries are made, and thus enables society to know where it is going and what it ought to do or not to do according to the projects, the hopes or the fears that it nurses.

To each stage of the growth of human society correspond ideas and beliefs that were obviously always latent, in varying degrees of strength, and that at certain moments become pre-eminent as correctives or additives to the social, political and economic state of this society, and as elements of its ethos. These ideas and beliefs are part of the human mind, and therefore part of the language which, up to a point, is the mind, the memory and the being of human kind. Irrespective of its linguistic differences, Europe is, in terms of thought and basic being or *logos*, one single entity rooted in Graeco-Judaic thought and beliefs which have been woven according to ethnological and historical differences into its various languages. Like works of art, the writings of Plato, the great Greek tragedies and the Bible have not remained fixed in the past; they have moved apace with the

87

growth of Western European society and they go on growing, and projecting themselves towards the future, and contributing to the making of the future. The philosophy of Plato, which has continuously changed throughout the ages, is as alive as the Venus de Milo or the Madonnas of Da Vinci, simply because with the philosopher as well as with the artist or the poet, language is not used as a means of communication, a coin or sign for an exchange which, once concluded, is absorbed into it, but as an organic entity incorporating ideas, thoughts and feelings aimed not at communication of meaning, but at revealing a complex and essential state of being, which remains ever ready to be apprehended by different individual sensibilities or beings, in a manner appropriate to the time and place, and is therefore a source of continuous creativity.

Great philosophy partakes of this continuous creativity; that is why we cannot define Plato, dream of fixing him or of giving him a once-and-for-all form which will never alter. Such an operation is impossible; we do not know and cannot know where exactly Plato begins or where he will end. His date of birth means nothing, it merely refers to his body as the receptacle of his thoughts; yet his thoughts are precisely what matters, and we do not exactly know where they came from. From Socrates? Heraclitus? Pythagoras? And others? Are they an emanation of what is perennial in the Greek psyche? How did the man Plato weld them together into the system that bears his name, and has gone on being altered, moulded, transformed, by Aristotle, Augustine, Descartes, Hegel, Husserl, Bergson, etc., etc., and will go on being ceaselessly transformed, so that we can never give it a final shape or form—for if we did, it would mean that it had nothing more to offer to the world, and that after twenty-five centuries of transformations, refutations and additions, it is finally dead?

A great philosopher's thought, and consequently a great philosophical system, is never finished, never closed, because its creator, its maker never had the time to close it according to his lights. God or Death always did that before he had time to think that the moment had come to do so. Plato, Descartes and Kant were all caught before they had said their last word, and so we continue to prolong the argument they left unfinished because their philosophy, like the *Iliad*, the *Odyssey* or *King Lear*, is a window opening on vast horizons, through which man can look and, according to his position in time or the height of his mind, see new lands and the coming forth of new metamorphoses.

Plato's essentialism, in the sense that he looked upon essences or ideas as being the perfect and true reality, is the natural philosophical antithesis to the Judaic emphasis on the importance of the here and now, to Marxist and Sartrian insistence upon existence, praxis and history, and to Kierkegaard's subjectivism and Heidegger's stress upon the importance of existence and *Dasein*. Plato's notion of looking upon life as made of moving shadows projected by light onto the walls of the cave, or upon existence as worthless froth or foam on the fringe of the Ocean of Eternity, is for superficial aspects of existentialism a notion that must be dethroned and replaced by something more concrete that places man and existence at the centre of creation. This is of course a gross over-simplification of Platonism which contains more wisdom within the bounds of its vision than any other philosophy has ever been able to muster, to say nothing of the fact that essentialism and existentialism are not and cannot be opposed, but are on the contrary coeval. There never is anything absolutely new in life, and existentialism has very deep roots which go back, if only partially, to its apparently antithetical attitude—essentialism, and without any doubt to its positive basis which is Socratism, or to the aspect of Socratic philosophy which insists upon the fact that to know is first and foremost to know oneself, and to behave normally is to be prepared to sacrifice one's own existence for the concrete truth in which one believes. Still, though Platonism looks upon the passage from the world of essences to that of existence as a fall, not unlike the Biblical fall, or a diminution caused by fragmented materialisation, the question of essence is very important, for, as we shall see later, the uses that Sartre makes of this word have nothing much to do with the use made of it by Plato and by idealist philosophers.

For Plato, nothing can exist but by participation in the essences of the intelligible world, the world of Ideas as immutable, necessary, perfect and eternal. Therefore they are the criteria by

which one can measure the distance between perfection and the
manifestations of existence which, being merely derived from
fragmented essence, are extremely limited in every respect,
including those of knowledge and morality, and which can only
be determined by comparison with, or reintegration into,
essence's perfection, reminiscences of which linger in the memory
of the existent's soul which, having been detached from essence,
is destined to return to it. It is easy to see how these philosophical
structures also underlie the structures of the Christian world
which, in its early stage, in the stage when it was oppressed and
crushed by Roman power, was, one might say, naturally Platonic
or neo-Platonic. Its triumph over Roman power, which it
defeated from within, marks with St Augustine the return of the
importance of existence in creation. The great mystery of the
incarnation thus began to shed its light on all men. Christ's life,
Christ's message, obscured and muffled by the sorrows and
suffering of a hounded people, began to be fully understood, and
understood by a people who soon became the ruling power. The
world, God's creation through the *logos*, appeared as informed
with His wisdom, and through Grace connected with Him.
Plato's intelligible world of Ideas became the world of God Who
has made Himself part of time, through His incarnation in
Christ, and thus shows the vital importance of the body and of
existence. The world is real, informed throughout with God's
subsistent essence; personal life is important, and man bears the
sense of his responsibility and the capacity, through his behaviour,
to reach the city of God. Of course, he cannot know the truth
except through his reference to God, therefore through his union
with Being, but truth is no longer a matter of mnemonic
reminiscences, it is a matter of love and light through Christ
and God Who speaks to us through conscience, that is to say
through the inner *I*.

Aristotle rejected Plato's intelligible world and replaced the
Ideas or essences which form this intelligible world with concepts
—general notions and attributes abstracted from things under
observation. Knowledge, in that respect, is basically observational
and consists in conceptualisations and interconnections between
universals. The human mind abstracts the universals from particulars which it has perceived through the senses. Thomas

Aquinas, Aristotle's commentator, adapted and modified a good deal of the latter's philosophy in the light of his own faith. For him, the existent comprises a form that could be either part of the Platonic idea or the essence which is part of God's creative essence, plus matter, which realises itself through, and according to, its form. Existence is therefore important, since it is informed with God's subsistent essence and connects human reason and individuated essence with the Absolute or Being which retains its primacy. The awareness of existence is the awareness of the relationship of the creature with his Creator, and the awareness of the limitations that separate two infinites. This awareness became more and more a source of anxiety with the Calvinists and the Jansenists, until it reached its most accomplished and telling formulation with Pascal who, more than anyone else, anticipates Kierkegaard and the main tenets of existentialism, which cannot, by any stretch of the imagination, be confined to Sartre's definition of it.

Pascal's tension or *Angst* between two infinites, that is to say between the infinitely small, inconsequential, yet thinking reed which is man, and the infinite of the cosmos which surrounds him and keeps eternally silent to all his questionings, led him to the choice of, or the leap into, faith and to the continuous anxiety that some sudden and, by definition, unforeseeable lack of Divine grace might cut him off for ever from salvation. This metaphysical anxiety that man feels in the face of the infinite and the unfathomable mystery of his existence, cannot be transformed into the inchoate and superficial notion of the absurd which enables Sisyphus to perform his hopeless task and yet to manage to derive satisfaction or some kind of vague happiness from the suffering imposed upon him by fate or by indifferent gods. Pascal asserts against Descartes' belief in mathematical truth the belief in astonishment in the face of existence, and the vital importance of the truth of the heart. Maine de Biran echoes his views, and from Pascal's truth of the heart to Kierkegaard's there is no distance at all, except in the mistaken notion of looking upon the latter as the knight in armour who shattered Hegel's idealistic edifice. This is a view that can be entertained only if one ignores the early Hegel before 1807, when he was deeply concerned with the role of the individual in society and in relation to others, and concentrates on the absolutism of the later Hegel.

Hegel's system is the triumph of reason. It is the crowning of the idealistic structure of the mind-world relationship that runs through Plato, Descartes, Leibniz and Kant before culminating in his attempt to bridge the gap between finite and infinite, being and Being, by leaping over it. Hegel marks the turning-point: after him came the new philosophical attitudes of Comte, Marx, Kierkegaard, Dostoyevsky, Nietzsche, Bergson, Husserl, Heidegger and Merleau-Ponty, to say nothing of Sartre. Hegel's name, like that of Plato, can never be ignored, for he is both an end and a beginning of all the metamorphoses of philosophy, including some of the most modern aspects of human knowledge, such as anthropology, psychology and linguistics.

Kierkegaard inaugurates the cult of subjectivity as the only basis of truth. This subjectivity cannot be understood in isolation, but only in relation with others, with God for those who believe in Him, and with the world to which all men necessarily belong. The relationship with the world is achieved through the body as the basis of perceiving and thinking, and existence is the means by which the world is known. Existence is consciousness. 'One cannot speak of existence apart from objects presented in immediate relationship to a consciousness,' says Gabriel Marcel (*Journal Métaphysique*, Gallimard, 1927, p. 18) This is a somewhat Berkeleyan view which might not rally all existentialists; far from it. But Marcel's existentialism is neither that of Sartre nor that of Merleau-Ponty whose realistic philosophy of the world could not subscribe to a notion such as: 'The universe tends to become abolished in proportion to the extent that it submerges us.' (Gabriel Marcel, *Du Refus à l'Invocation*, Gallimard, 1940, p. 32) The main concern of existentialism is with the concrete, with the substance of things which becomes the non-mediated data of consciousness. This implies a rejection of abstraction and systematic thinking, which is merely conceptual and, as Bergson pointed out, deals merely with the surface of things.

Therefore existentialist philosophy, from Kierkegaard onwards, tends to avoid and, even more, repudiate systematic exposition and prefers to express itself in journals, essays, fiction, plays and all forms of writing directly connected with personal life. Heidegger's *Being and Time* and Sartre's *L'Etre et le Néant* are exceptions; and *L'Etre et le Néant* is in many ways unsatisfactory, incomplete and, at times, at odds with the philosophical views embodied in Sartre's plays. Yet, how could it be otherwise, when the main tenet of existentialism is to shun abstractions and systematic concepts, to return to things themselves, and to try to capture the real flux of the inner life, the non-mediated data of consciousness, before intellect intervenes and introduces separations, categorisations and generalisations which this flux does not and cannot inherently possess? Thus Sartre's dualistic notions of the *in-se* and the *per-se*, of the self and the other, are conceptual notions, which cut across Sartre's basic purpose, and distort his researches from the start. He remains Cartesian, notwithstanding his protestations, and we shall see that there are in his philosophy other more irreconcilable or antithetical notions, like that of Being and Nothingness, together with a lack of coherence in his notion of freedom and choice.

5

Atheistic Existentialism: Jean-Paul Sartre

Philosopher, political and literary essayist, novelist and play-wright, Sartre (b. 1905) has achieved a world-wide reputation in each of these disciplines. The success of his popularisations of existentialism in short and readable essays, like *L'Existentialisme est un Humanisme*, through his novels and through his plays, which have an important philosophical content, because Sartre is above all a philosopher-*littérateur*, and because some of them are among the great plays of the twentieth century, will have to be discussed very briefly in the course of this study which is primarily concerned with philosophy. Whether it is because existentialism is more a philosophical attitude to life than a philosophy, or because it is by nature impossible to systematise it, the fact is that Sartre's attempt to do so in *L'Etre et le Néant* is not entirely satisfactory, and his attempts at simplification and vulgarisation, like *L'Existentialisme est un Humanisme* and his various essays and dramas, have produced some notorious tag phrases and some over-simplified descriptions which do not quite correspond to the realities of the philosophical problems involved. The philosophical notion of existentialism necessarily implies a certain primacy of existence, but primacy over what, and in what way? That is a question that is difficult to answer. Is it primacy over the other current term of the diptych which is essence? Is it primacy in time? Such questions land us straight in the middle of purely intellectual debates or mental abstractions which existentialism, by definition, purports to avoid. Yet it is exactly what Sartre does when, for instance, he states : 'There is one being whose existence precedes essence, a being which exists before it can be defined by any conception of it. . . . Man is nothing but what he makes of himself . . . in choosing for him-

94

self, he chooses for the whole of mankind.' (*L'Existentialisme est un Humanisme*, Nagel, 1946, pp. 21–24) Or : 'Man without support or help is condemned at each instant to invent man', (*ibid.*, p. 38) or : 'The whole of the eighteenth century believed that there was an essence common to all men, which they called *human nature*. Existentialism maintains, on the contrary, that with man—and with man alone—existence precedes essence. This means, more simply, that man *is*, and that afterwards he is this or that.' (*Action*, 12th December, 1944)

I should not dream of doubting Sartre's intellectual capacity to see clearly by himself the weakness and the speciousness of the statements here quoted, yet be that as it may, they sum up some of the most important aspects of what could be described as Sartre's philosophical puzzles. He knows perfectly well that the philosophical concepts of existence and essence cannot be spatially or temporally separated, that there is not a philosophical entity called essence which, God knows how, is seized and used in order to make existence. Sartre knows that the equation of essence with the notion of an ideal ens or form from which a concrete or organic unity is made, whether this entity is Fontenelle's melon, a human being or a piece of furniture, is not valid and is not in fact what is meant by essence. The notion of universals as sources of the existence of particulars is a discredited notion not even worth discussing. Sartre knows perfectly well that the metaphysical notion of essence, that is to say the notion of essence as the subsistence of existence, is by definition timeless, and that therefore it is not possible to order these two notions in time, and least of all to make of essence an emanation from existence, for this kind of emanation is no longer metaphysical essence or form, but a concept—the concept which is obtained from abstractions of the various qualities and actions of a given human life and which can be said to sum up or to represent the schema, graph or ashes of this human life. This concept, which Sartre tries to camouflage as an essence purely for the good of his cause, has nothing to do with essence as emanation of Being.

Essence and existence can only be coeval, though not co-extensive. Essence with a capital 'E' is the creativity, the force, the sum of virtualities that make life and existence possible, for it stands to reason that existence could not be unless it were possible, that is to say unless one posits a creativity which is intent upon existence. This creativity is Essence or Being which individuates itself in various forms of organic or inorganic existence and which, therefore, is coeval with existence which is its actualisation in time. So that it is nonsense to say : 'I construct the world; in the least of my acts I commit the whole of mankind'—perhaps not quite nonsense, but merely high-flown though admittedly well-meaning rhetoric, or merely what Verlaine pejoratively described as 'littérature'. For how can one single individual who lives in a world, or in a context of life in which the notion of human nature, that is to say the notion of basic human similarities of needs, origins and finality, is explicitly repudiated, involve the whole of mankind through any one of his actions? This is certainly a grandiose, awe-inspiring notion of the importance of human responsibility, but as a philosophical notion it cannot be integrated into what is at the start, according to Sartre, a monadic world of spontaneous generation of existence and of freedom. For who can co-ordinate this extraordinary primeval luxuriance? No-one; no God, of course, since He is dead; nothing remains, except Sartre's mind engaged once more in the Hegelian task of being God, or the god of his time : 'Man is the being who plans to be God;' (*L'Etre et le Néant*, Gallimard, 1943, p. 653); or : 'Man desires to be God.' (*Ibid.*, p. 654)

If man desires to be God, he surely must begin by recognising the rational fact that God put at least a little more coherence than he is credited with into the world that He is supposed to have created. Without falling into the common trap of superficial determinism, guided finality and what not, which are usual aunt sallies of those who want to maintain at all costs, and oblivious of Spinoza's warning, a notion of untrammelled existential freedom, it ought to be rational to acknowledge by now the existence of a straightforward biological or metaphysical teleology which is strictly confined to the actualisation of the biological or the essential and basic properties of the component elements of life, and which has nothing to do with guiding hands or pointing fingers constantly interfering with a highly elusive notion of human freedom.

The notion of freedom together with that of nothingness with which it is inextricably connected, constitute perhaps the most unsatisfactory aspect of Sartre's philosophy. As an exalting, humanitarian concept of individual responsibility and moral duty, Sartre's gropings towards a definition of freedom are admirable and deserve applause, but this should not disguise the fact that a close examination of their philosophical structures cannot but reveal their underlying contradictions and their lack of coherence. To say this is merely to acknowledge the fact that he has not succeeded in doing what nobody else has yet done, that is, to give a metaphysical foundation to freedom. This could be done only by grounding it in Being, and for this, one would have to be either a Christian or a metaphysician, and Sartre is neither, so that he has undertaken with materialistic and psycho-analytical concepts to produce what amounts to a metaphysical definition of freedom. 'Man makes himself and in making himself makes the world.' Having said this, he has to concede that 'man is simply a situation . . . entirely conditioned by his class, his salary, the nature of his work, conditioned even to his emotional attitudes and his ideas.' (*Les Temps Modernes*, 1st October, 1945) Marx would not have spoken otherwise. Man is therefore severely limited not only by his situation in the world, but also by his physical conditions and his economic background. If he is lame, half blind, mentally deficient or worse, his freedom will be curtailed still more by these physical limitations. Sartre's answer to this state of affairs is well known and again leads to all sorts of inconclusive arguments and practically impossible riddles. 'We are choice, and to be is for us to choose . . . I cannot be an invalid without having chosen the way in which I regard my infirmity as humiliating, intolerable, to be hidden, to be exhibited as a source of pride or as a justification of failure.' (*L'Etre et le Néant*, p. 393) And so on. There is a great deal of truth in the latter part of this statement and there is, above all, the basis of an ethic of moral courage and forbearance in order to transcend the weaknesses and diminutions that are part of the human lot. But this commendable appeal to human stoicism, to the courage to take on fully the calamities and failings that befall man, can neither be pushed too far, nor can it, above all, be confused with freedom.

We are no doubt free to weep or not to weep; that is purely a freedom of response to a given situation, but we are not free

F.T.—G

to create or not create this situation, and that is the crucial point. We are free in our reactions to it, but our freedom is a mental act, an act that could transform, if we wished, the chains we carry as burdens round our necks into imaginary and beautifying necklaces. Nevertheless, the chains remain, and while some men will no doubt applaud our heroism, others will gently smile at our credulity and at our capacity to transform the harsh facts of life into wishful thinking. One cannot but be on the side of those who will always admire the courage of human beings who can turn their sores into acceptances and joys, or who can still smile even when the knife is at their throats. But turning from the plane of noble sentiments onto which Sartre has, as he very often does, led us, to the harsh plane of philosophy, we are compelled to realise that things are, as far as freedom is concerned, different from the way he would like them to be. 'We mean,' he says, 'that man first of all exists, encounters himself, emerges into the world and defines himself afterwards. If man as the existentialist sees him is not definable, it is because to begin with he is nothing.' (*L'Existentialisme est un Humanisme*, p. 21) This is the hub of Sartre's philosophical problem, which concerns the range and meaning of the notion of nothingness, a notion that Sartre has vaguely suggested he will explore further; yet as he has not done so, one must deal with what he offers, and what he offers does not seem to be quite satisfactory.

It must be said at the outset that this is one of the most vital problems of philosophy, if not *the* most vital; it is the problem of the relationship between Being and nothingness; it has not been solved, or perhaps it cannot be solved, and it is certainly not solved by Sartre's dualism and near equation of the two terms. Man is nothing, liberty is absence, negativity nothingness, and existence, which is the receptacle or instrument of this liberty, is also nothingness, which must somehow, as nothingness, become part of being, in order to be a *Dasein* in a world which exists, and in which this being-there exercises his freedom, which is nothingness. First of all the notion of nothingness as a substratum, therefore as a shadowy entity upon which being feeds and from which it emerges into existence, is too obviously unmanageable to be accepted. As the rightfully irate King Lear said to an obstinate Cordelia: 'Nothing will come of nothing';

one can also say that nothing cannot be the source or the basis of something. Sartre makes the mistake over and over again, a mistake that Heidegger does not make : he attempts to turn nothingness into an entity, something which is, in fact, a pseudo-idea, for nothingness cannot be given any predicative capacity without producing an impossible dualism in all aspects of life. Nothingness can only be part of, or a by-product of being, but it cannot be the basis of being, or of freedom. The fact that freedom implies a nihilating activity is quite another matter, but it must be remembered that it does so, not in order to be subtilised into nothingness, but in order to manifest or to express being, for without being there could not be any existence, and I stress the fact that I do not say : 'there would only be nothingness', for nothingness cannot be.

Yet moving away from the simplifications of *L'Existentialisme est un Humanisme* to *L'Etre et le Néant*, Sartre recognises the fact that nothingness is not to be equated with being, but is on the contrary inherent in being, 'and lies at the heart of being like a worm'. This would be a fair enough description, but when it comes to the workings and attributes of nothingness, nothingness is again given predicative attributes that make of this notion an entity. Nothingness annihilates itself or nihilates itself, or is nihilated, so that, whatever way nothingness is dealt with, it is given an entity status. The being that has the capacity to nihilate nothingness and also to sustain nothingness is man, who, according to Sartre, is a being through whom nothingness comes into the world; being itself is a 'lack', a kind of nothingness. One can see at once how this kind of circuitous argument is unsatisfactory, and it is above all unsatisfactory because Sartre uses philosophical terms more as concrete terms, parts of everyday linguistic imagery, than as purely philosophical concepts. The terms 'nothingness' and 'nihilation' are closer in the usual Sartrian meaning to the concept of absence, unrealised possibilities and negation of everything except the existing or sought-after presence, than to the philosophical concepts they refer to. Human beings are necessarily compounds of positivities and negations, syntheses carrying 'lacks' or absences of what has not been and yet might have been, and also have to face the nothingness of the future which is also freedom. In the face of this nothingness confronting consciousness continuously nihilating some of its own being—all the possibilities that are rejected—the result is necessarily continuous anguish. But the point that causes difficulty is that nothingness is made into something, a something which is nothing and which always confronts consciousness. Therefore this concept of nothingness is untenable, as untenable as the one that equates it with absence, emptiness, lack of a presence whose absence becomes a nothingness, *un néant*, which annihilates everything around this absence of a longed-for presence, as is the case with the search in a café for an absent friend called Pierre, which Sartre quotes in *L'Etre et le Néant* (p. 9) in order to illustrate his theory.

The trouble with Sartre's systematic philosophy is that having disposed of God, basis of all values, uncaused cause of absence and existence, he has attempted to make his notion of nothingness perform all these various tasks. Existence and freedom, which are, in fact, with him, synonymous, have to be equated with nothingness, and this is an operation that no linguistic sleight of hand, no verbal skill, however great, can perform, for there is no true logic in the argument. All the attempts to order essence and existence, and essence and freedom, are purely artificial word-plays and, as such, meaningless. From Leibniz to modern biology, it is clearly understood that it is not possible to think of the notion of a pre-life in order to prepare for and to organise life, any more than it is possible to think of a pre-being which would prepare for and organise being.

The problem is simple, and Sartre no doubt sees it more clearly than most, but it does not suit his moral preoccupations, his political views, his creative aptitudes or—who knows?—perhaps his psychological ethos, to accept it. Perhaps he does not wish to accept the notion of a being or life which is caused by the properties that are an inherent part of its essence. Perhaps he does not wish to accept the notion of a Being which is because its essence—the force that animates it—is to be, or life as being the outcome of the properties of its component elements which possess their own evolutive creativity. So he peremptorily declares that: 'Being is, without reason, without cause and without necessity' (*L'Etre et le Néant*, p. 713) or that: 'All existing beings are born without reason, continue through weakness, and die by accident.' (*La Nausée*, Gallimard, 1938, p. 170) This is, of course, pure rhetoric, which may produce a temporary dazzle but cannot carry conviction, for it is, throughout, a denial of logic. Being is, and can only be for exactly the reason for which Sartre denies its reality. As for existing beings, there are certainly reasons for their being in the world; one of them, good enough, is the pure and simple biological reproduction urge; while the continuation of beings through weakness is merely the kind of paradox in which Sartre indulges, unless of course he alludes to their mental weakness, that is to say to the average individual's incapacity to commit suicide. When it comes to dying by accident, we are faced again with an untruth; we all die by design, that of our birth, and if Sartre had, like Heidegger, accepted death as an essential and absolute part of life, he could have avoided such levities.

Still, it is the notion of freedom that underlies, in my view, the most irreconcilable contradictions between Sartre's moral aspirations and his metaphysical phobias. 'Man,' he says, 'could not be sometimes free, sometimes slave; he is always and totally free, or he is not' (*L'Etre et le Néant*, p. 516); 'freedom is an unanalysable totality.' (*Ibid.*, p. 529) We are back to Kant's noumenal notion of freedom, without of course accepting, like Kant, the notion of a noumenon or thing in itself, which is part of the world of essence. 'We are freedom which chooses; we do not choose to be free. We are condemned to freedom.' (*Ibid.*, p. 565) Or: 'Freedom is freedom to choose, but not freedom not to choose. Not to choose, in fact, is to choose not to choose. . . . In consequence choice is the basis of the being chosen but not the basis of the act of choosing. Hence the absurdity of freedom.' (*Ibid.*, p. 561) So we are condemned to be free; freedom is therefore not free choice, but pure and simple necessity when it is not nothingness, and we are condemned to an absurd existence, since existence is freedom. Freedom, which is indeed indefinable, has been equated with necessity, or with the awareness or the consciousness of being, something which carries a character of necessity in all idealistic systems of philosophy. Sartre, who basically repudiates idealism, tries to establish what he would call existential causes of freedom, which are partly analogous to the Indian rope trick, in that he attempts to base freedom on nothing, and partly a reiteration of Doctor Coué's method, in that he aims at convincing us that we are free, whether we like it or not, and that being condemned to be free, we might as well accept our sentence with good grace and pretend that we have really asked for it, for we are not only free for ourselves, but also for others and because of others. But are we really free? Certainly not, and Sartre himself says so: 'Conscious deliberation is always fake. . . . When I deliberate, the choice is already made. And if I have to undertake to deliberate, it is merely because it is part of my original project to take into account my motives through *deliberation*, rather than by any other form of discovery. By the time the will comes into play, the decision has already been taken, the will's function is merely to announce it.' (*Ibid.*, p. 527)

Choice makes itself through thinking, which consists merely in the emergence into consciousness of the choice made. We do not make it, we only know it; but then, why pretend? Sartre clearly acknowledges this fact and recognises that our choices are the result of subterranean, indefinable processes which are not wilfully made, but which could, up to a point, be traced back to certain sources, analysed and made to serve as mirrors of what is called our personality. Such an analysis will of course show that there are certain reasons why we have made a given choice, but we did not know them *a priori*, and therefore we cannot say that we used them in order to make the choice, for these reasons made themselves what they are, through the choice; yet, they are nevertheless reasons, and in spite of that Sartre does not hesitate to declare that the choice is absolutely free, 'made without any basis,' (*ibid.*, p. 558), or that: 'it is founded on no good reason for the good reason that all reason comes into the world by free choice.' (*Ibid.*, p. 567) All reason, all values come into the world by free choice, but then where does free choice come from? No answer is possible, for the argument looks like a dazzling transcendental wheel rolling in space, having come from nowhere and going nowhere; we can only gaze at it in amazement, as we do at various other Sartrian pronouncements on this topic. 'The choice is bound to be one and the same as the consciousness that we have of ourselves.' (*Ibid.*, p. 539) But how do we know if this consciousness of ourselves is consciousness of our true self, for we are always what we think we are not, and we are never truly what we think we are? How can consciousness as nothingness ever be aware of a self to which it could refer as the true self, which is the measure of authentic actions and behaviour? And this problem is complicated by the fact that Sartre considers the past as an in-itself, dead and completely separated from the for-itself, therefore we have a for-itself without any basis whatsoever (to say nothing of an impossible dualism at the heart of the notion of consciousness), while this for-itself is freedom, which for Sartre is 'a perpetual escape from contingency, it is interiorisation, nihilation and subjectivisation of contingency, a return to the surge of primitive absurdity.' (*Ibid.*, p. 559) 'It is because human reality is not enough that it is free; freedom is a lack of being, a nothingness.' (*Ibid.*, p. 516)

Freedom is nothingness, our choices are spontaneous and unexplainable; they could therefore be anything, and the problem of knowing whether they are morally good or bad sets Sartre new problems which he seeks to avoid by more circular arguments. Our choices are born in anguish and overburden us with a sense of responsibility to all men, for everything that happens in the world. In a way, this is no doubt true; there is human solidarity, and in one way or another we cannot avoid our responsibility for the war in Vietnam or for the destruction of the Jews; but then we cannot say that our choices are absurd and completely irrational manifestations of individual existences, deprived of any all-embracing truths such as community of needs, aspirations, similarity of beginnings and ends, in fact what is commonly called a human nature, something that Sartre denies as pertaining to the domain of essences. If we are responsible, as we are, for other men, then there must be some kind of rationality that embraces all men, and this rationality cannot be made by spontaneous, absurd individual choices that become sanctified by anguish and by the sense of responsibility conferred upon them. These choices must on the contrary conform to this rationality, to accepted norms of love, comprehension, tolerance, human brotherhood, born from the very essence of man, or at least from the millenary sedimentations of the human mind throughout its whole historical life, made possible by reason and language. Yet for Sartre 'man is placed in the necessity of choosing himself perpetually,' (*ibid.*, p. 560) and in doing so, he makes himself, and in making himself he assumes responsibility for the entire human race, for 'if there is neither value nor moral *a priori*, and if in each case we have to decide on our own, without guidance, yet for all men, how can we avoid feeling anxiety when we have to act? Every one of our acts involves the meaning of the world and man's place in it.' (*Action*, 12th December, 1944)

Needless to say, this anxiety and sense of responsibility when confronted with the making of choices are extremely subjective notions, as subjective as the notion of nausea and disgust at the so-called viscosity and deadness of things; they lead, of course, to the arbitrary notion of bad faith, which is for Sartre the refusal to acknowledge or to feel this nausea about the world, or the refusal to be, as in the unfortunate case of Baudelaire, what, according to Sartre, he truly was. But it is, alas, always Sartre or someone else who decides what X or Y truly is, and the reasons why he should feel nausea about the world. Yet Sartre himself acknowledges the fact that man cannot know what he truly is, since he is never what he thinks he is, so how can man—this unfathomed, uncharted instrument—make use of himself to measure and ascertain what another truly is, and whether his life is or is not 'authentic'? He obviously can only impose his subjective values on the actions and behaviour of the individual whom he tries to assess, and pass upon him arbitrary judgments based on subjectively apprehended appearances. Thus Baudelaire was a decadent bourgeois obsessed by sin, by the lost security of his childhood world destroyed by his mother's marriage to the dreadful General Aupick, and who, unconcerned by the world about him, took refuge in the writing of poetry as a useless passion or as a means of escape. In fact he failed to be what Sartre would have liked him to be—a committed writer, a defender of worthy causes, a destroyer of sham bourgeois morality. Flaubert seemed to suffer from the same failings, and Sartre psychoanalyses himself through him as he did through Baudelaire; the result is interesting psychoanalysis and a widening knowledge of the ever fascinating Sartrian personality, but in the case of Baudelaire, for instance, it has nothing much to do with literary criticism, or with the poet who wrote some of the most beautiful poetry ever written.

L'Etre et le Néant presents an ontology, a search for being that precedes or underlies any kind of questioning as to what it is. Sartre distinguishes between two modes of being—being-in-itself, that is to say being which coincides with itself, which is therefore dead, past, closed, finished, etc.; and being-for-itself—consciousness—which is an active process introducing nothingness into being by nihilating the in-itself. 'The for-itself is indeed nothing but the total nihilation of the in-itself. . . . The for-itself possesses no other reality than that of being the nihilation of being.' (*L'Etre et le Néant*, pp. 711–12) This dualism between the in-itself as not-being and the for-itself as the activity that brings nothingness into being, seems to me artificial and unreal. While it is true to say with Sartre that the world is what we make it, and that without being Berkeleyan to the point of saying *esse est percipi*, we can agree that things acquire their meaning through consciousness, it does not seem possible to divide being into an entity that has neither meaning nor purpose nor attributes, called the 'in-itself', and a project-making, exploring, forward-moving 'for-itself'. The terminology does not justify the conclusion drawn from Sartre's use of it. 'For-itself' implies that there is an 'itself', a something which is aimed at, and a force or a movement which aims at the reaching of this 'itself'. This psychological entity, whatever it is, cannot be made to surge endlessly and repeatedly from a nihilated in-itself, that is to say from nothing. One never has the suggested Sartrian awareness of being born absolutely anew, freshly minted and free from any accretions. One is never free from one's own past which, contrary to what Sartre suggests, is not a dead in-itself, but a latent texture of the inner *I* or for-itself which is consciousness. Consciousness is not a leap forward, or rather 'forward' is the wrong word, for it implies a direction, a teleonomy of some kind, while for Sartre it is a cricket-like leap into space to land anywhere, having started from nowhere or, as he says, from nothingness; it can only be, on the contrary, an awareness of the true being of things and of Being, apprehended by the essential subjectivity becoming aware of its existence as a duration involving necessarily its past and future grasped synchronically as a living present, and this is something that cannot be conceived of in dualistic Sartrian terms of 'in-itself' and 'for-itself', for these terms are aspects of the mind knowing itself as a knowing self in the act of knowing.

For Sartre, consciousness has nothing substantial about it, it is pure 'appearance', in the sense that 'it only exists in so far as is becomes apparent to itself.' (*Ibid.*, p. 23) This is equivalent to Husserl's view that consciousness is an intentionality and that it is always consciousness of something. But this intentionality, whatever it is, cannot be reduced to Sartre's conclusion that: 'The for-itself is the nothing by means of which there are things.' (*Ibid.*, p. 230) Clearly, consciousness is not the Cartesian *ego*, but it is not an in-itself and it is not a nothing, so it must be a latency of being, a being that carries in itself the possibility of being other than itself, so that this latent possibility might reveal itself or reveal its being in privileged moments of coincidence between the desire for being-in-itself and its emergence as being-for-itself—a truly God-like moment. The consciousness of the for-itself is a very complex problem : 'The for-itself, in so far as it is not *itself*, is a presence to itself that lacks a certain presence to itself, and it is the lack of this presence that makes of it a presence to itself.' (*Ibid.*, p. 145) Consciousness supposes therefore a lack, a void, a nothingness at its heart, a nothingness which is the very proof that it is not an in-itself. Consciousness creates nothingness and this proves that it is not nothingness. 'The for-itself is a being for which its being is by nature in question, in as far as this being is essentially a mode of *not being* a being that is envisaged at the same time as other than itself.' (*Ibid.*, p. 222) Consciousness's nihilating power becomes understandable, I think, if one looks upon it as the Mallarméan imagination having the ability to abolish or nullify the real so as to replace it by the imaginary, which is the sensation or the experience transformed into or replaced by its imaginative equivalence, in which consciousness, aware of itself and also aware of its creativeness, is entirely subsumed in the result of this creativity which is the poem.

When Sartre transfers his extraordinary analytical power and psychological insight from abstract philosophising to concrete subjects and to the study of literary creation and the working of the imagination, as in *L'Imaginaire* (Gallimard, 1940), the results are remarkably interesting, for now the abstract terminology which makes his philosophical cogitations at times so difficult to follow or to accept, finds its true concrete basis and its illuminating validity. We easily know here what is really meant by the 'nullifying' gaze of a person who looks for someone who is not in the place where he is being looked for. But the nihilation of the in-itself in order to make possible the rise of the for-itself is another matter, yet Sartre says: 'The for-itself arises out of the nihilation of the in-itself and this takes the form of a projection towards the in-itself; between this nihilated in-itself and the projected in-itself, the for-itself is nothing.' (*Ibid.*, pp. 652–53) So we have the in-itself nihilated, separated by nothing from a for-itself aimed at nothing; we have in fact a for-itself made to rest on nothing and, strictly speaking, directed at nothing. This seems rather difficult to understand; the only supposition one could make is that the for-itself which is the nihilated in-itself becomes, if or when it achieves fusion with the in-itself that it is aimed at, a closed totality or transcendence—a notion that Sartre repudiates. Altogether, we seem to be faced with a vague concept of an uncaused being which, in Mallarméan fashion, goes from nihilated reality, that is to say from nowhere, to nowhere, and is nothing but the duration of this going between nothingness and nothingness. The outcome of this attempt to place being between two nothingnesses is that: 'Human reality is by nature sick because it comes into being as perpetually haunted by a totality which it cannot be, simply because it cannot reach being-in-itself without ceasing to be being-for-itself.' (*Ibid.*, p. 134) The for-itself seems to be infinite freedom surging from nothingness —a nihilating activity having no teleonomy (which would be antinomic to it) and yet, in the end, seeming to have a purpose or an aim. There is a lack of total coincidence between the being of the for-itself and its phenomenal appearing, that is to say the for-itself which is supposed to be projection towards the in-itself, and the in-itself which should be absolutely nihilated, for this in-itself is not absolutely reduced to nothing, but obviously leaves something indefinable or transcendental, which is the projection or projecting force of the for-itself, a force that Sartre describes with the words: 'Human reality is pure effort to become God, without any foundation given to this effort, or without there being *anything* which strives thus; the desire expresses this effort.'

(*Ibid.*, p. 664) So man is a useless passion, is condemned, in principle, to an absurd existence; I say 'in principle', for Sartre does not apply his doctrine to himself, and in fact the *Critique de la Raison Dialectique* (1960) vigorously endeavours to correct this notion of the uselessness of life by attempting to integrate existentialism into Marxism.

Before coming to this work, I should like to examine briefly one of the central notions of Sartre's philosophy, the notion of the other. The notorious tag phrase connected with this aspect of Sartre's philosophy is well known : 'Hell is other people', a sentence that expresses the theme of one of his plays, *Huis Clos*. Then there are other such tag phrases : 'My original fall is the existence of the other.' (*L'Etre et le Néant*, p. 321) 'I must turn the others into objects before they turn me into an object. . . . The gaze of the others steals the world from me, empties the world.' (*Ibid.*, p. 322) The gaze of the others, like Medusa's gaze, turns everything to stone and makes of the world a desert; communion of souls is impossible. The touch of the other person is unbearable. The universe is nothing but a constant menace, and things have a repellency, a viscosity which creates a sense of horror analogous to that caused by the presence of the most terrifying beasts. To be aware of existence is to be aware of a revulsion against existence, for existence is mercilessly stifled by matter and by its proliferation of things. Existence is a Mallarméan nightmare of feeling imprisoned in ice or of growing paralysis and transformation into the in-itself of things.

This type of reaction to things can only be a paranoiac reaction, as paranoiac as the sense of shame one is supposed to have at the awareness that 'you is what the other makes you'. The look of the other turns us into objects, and to look at them is to turn them into objects. To be seen by others amounts to a practical extinction of our own self. 'I am as the other sees me, . . . I am ashamed of myself as I appear to the other.' (*Ibid.*, p. 267) In page after page, in the chapter of *L'Etre et le Néant* entitled *The Look and the existence of the Other*, Sartre explains in detail the relationship of the subject with the other, and in reading these pages one cannot but be surprised at the horror and fear that the other seems to arouse in the thinking subject. This terror rests upon the basic fact that there is no *cogito*, that consciousness is nothingness which makes itself through things caught in the activity of the for-itself. 'I am my own nothingness. I am what I am not and I am not what I am. . . . I am nothing; there is only a pure nothingness surrounding and delineating a kind of objective whole set in the world. . . . Shame is shame of oneself, it is the recognition that I am the object which the other looks at and judges. . . . I can only be ashamed of my freedom in as far as it eludes me to become a given object.' (*Ibid.*, pp. 318–19)

Shame is the basis of bad faith; the look of the other empties me, dissolves me into the world, I cease to be myself, and I am reduced to that being which has been emptied of himself, thence my feeling of shame : 'the freedom of the other is revealed to me through the disquieting indetermination of the being that I am for him. . . . It looks as if I possessed a dimension of being from which I am separated by a radical nothingness : and this nothingness is the freedom of the other; the other must bring about my being-for-himself in as far as he has to be his being. . . . If there is another, whoever he may be, whatever may be his relations with me, without his acting upon me except through the pure emergence of his being, I have an appearance, I have a nature; my original fall is the existence of the other; and shame is like pride—the apprehension of myself as nature, even though that very nature eludes me and is unknowable as such. It does not quite mean that I am aware of the loss of my freedom to become a *thing*, but it is over there, out of my lived freedom, as an attribute given to the being that I am for the other.' (*Ibid.*, p. 321) We obviously have here an expression of hypersensibility to the outside world, and of a consciousness of the other that goes beyond any possible logical explanation, except as the manifestation of a very singular subjectivity which is as fearful of scrutiny by others or absorption by others as it is altruistic and generous in everyday life.

Sartre as a psychoanalyst sees the gaze as turned upon itself, therefore attempting to remain closed to any external penetration or interference. The other is repelled as an intruder, and is not accepted as a component element of the same world and situation, sharing in a horizontal transcendence. Sartre is psychologically locked up in his own vertical transcendence. He aspires upwards towards an absent God. The shame in the face of the other can only be inverted pride and desire for uniqueness, for the only shame one should have in front of the other is that of feeling inadequate and unable to do more for him, instead of fearing him and avoiding him as an enemy. One should be ashamed only of one's own limitations, but not of being looked at, judged, or turned into a thing-in-itself by the other. Yet Sartre insists that 'shame is the sense of *original fall*, not from the fact that I have committed this or that sin, but simply because I have *fallen* into the world . . . and that I need the mediation of another human being in order to be what I am.' (*Ibid.*, p. 349) True, man needs man, to be whatever he is, but in this case the other is not only a mediator, he is above all a constant threat, for in the Sartrian world there is no hope of togetherness, no hope of living alongside others in love and brotherhood in an Edenic or Rousseauesque universe. For him, man is not good at heart, and there is no hope that he will love his neighbour; he is locked up in himself, at war with every self around him, and he must either subdue or be subdued; he must be master or slave, subject or object, he must either realise his project or be mere project and a thing-in-itself for the other. 'One must either transcend the other or be transcended by him; the essence of relationship between consciousnesses is not *being with*, it is conflict.' (*Ibid.*, p. 502)

Love is no exception to this general rule of human strife. The lover desires to possess the other, not so much as an object or thing, but as a freedom, as a means of existing through him, and thus justifying his existence through him. This type of relationship being naturally self-defeating, it is difficult to see how love could be anything but the constant struggle of two consciousnesses, each endeavouring to use the other as stolen freedom in order to assert its own freedom. This freedom asserts itself by compelling the other to love the one who has taken his freedom from him, and therefore reduced him to a thing-in-itself. Once this aim has been achieved, once the lover's for-itself has absorbed or nihilated the other's in-itself, he has no other proof of his own existence, no other activity for his for-itself, and he must begin again, and so on and so on, unless of course someone reverses the roles and applies the same process to him. If, perchance, two lovers could pause in the middle of this type of strife and stabilise their relationship, their equilibrium could not last for long, for the love of a third person—Gorgon-like—would petrify them and destroy this equilibrium, so that they would have to begin again. One is always superfluous to another person, and therefore the presence of one single consciousness is enough to disturb the peace and, like the serpent in Eve's Garden of Eden, to introduce evil. 'Original fall is my appearance in a world where there is the other.' (Ibid., p. 481) The others, of course, feel the same way about me, so that, each feeling that he is the cause of the shame and of the sense of guilt of the other, to say nothing of the fear of nihilation by the other, men can only live in a state of alienation that makes of existence an absurdity or a continuous source of anxiety and terror. I cannot make myself without the other, I cannot see without being seen, I am always on the razor edge of being a freedom or a nothing-ness, and as freedom is nothingness, I do not get out of nothingness.

Could man find some distraction from his preoccupation with nothingness and shame through the desire for another human being? Certainly not, for desire is merely the incarnation of a consciousness in order to absorb the incarnation of the other's consciousness; it is a form of mental cannibalism; one consciousness-carrying body absorbs another: 'This is the true meaning of the word possession. It is certain that I want to possess the other's body, but I want to possess it only in so far as it is itself "possessed", that is, in so far as the other's consciousness is identified with his body.' (Ibid., p. 460) It is clear that once this possession has taken place, the for-itself ceases to work, for, the object of desire or attraction having been absorbed, only its shell or appearance remains, and this shell or appearance is an instrument or a thing, an in-itself. Similarly, any other form of human relationship from sadism to hatred can only end in frustration, for consciousness can neither be truly mediated by flesh, that is to say identified with it, nor made a pure epiphenomenon of it, therefore it can never be appropriated in any shape or form by another, it always eludes absorption or transformation into a thing-in-itself. This is all the more impos-sible in Sartre's world in which consciousness, moving from nothingness towards nothingness, is necessarily powerless to deal with any monadic pattern which repeats its own properties.

The Sartrian assertion that 'we are condemned to freedom' is a practical acceptance of the hopelessness and inanity of life in a world in which human relationships are reduced to conflict. The *Critique de la Raison Dialectique* is Sartre's attempt to correct the nihilistic idealism of *L'Etre et le Néant* and to give to Marxism a basis of existentialism which makes it possible to place man in the context of history and to look upon him, not as a 'useless passion', but as a meaningful participant in its making. It marks a return to the Husserlian search for the latent rationality of things, a rationality which is not mathematical and abstract, but apprehended in action by a subject bodily involved in the world, as a living being which is a centre of exchanges with all those who share with it the existential condition. Sartre has tried to meet some of the arguments raised by Merleau-Ponty in his review of *L'Etre et le Néant*, published under the title of *Querelles de l'Existentialisme*, in which he says : 'The only way to attain what philosophy seeks to attain—a complete apprehension of the world—is to join history instead of contemplating it. As Marx said in a famous text, the only way to realise philosophy is to destroy it.' (*Sens et Non-sens*, Nagel, 1963, p. 136) And Merleau-Ponty continues : 'Marxism not only tolerates liberty and the individual, but as a materialism it places upon man a kind of dizzy responsibility' (*ibid.*, p. 141); he concludes his article with words that Sartre seems to have taken to heart : 'A living Marxism should "save" the existentialist research and integrate it instead of stifling it." (*Ibid.*, p. 143) This can be done by widening the notion of class, for according to Merleau-Ponty, 'a given class cannot become an historical and revolutionary factor as long as its component elements are not conscious that they form a class.' (*Ibid.*, p. 139)

Sartre acknowledges the fact that the philosophy that dominates our time is Marxism, while existentialism is only an ideology—'a parasitic system which lives on the fringe of the knowledge to which it was first opposed, and into which it now endeavours to integrate itself.' (*Critique de la Raison Dialectique*, p. 18) Philosophical systems remain alive until history has actualised them. Marxism has not, by any account, been actualised yet. Another philosophy is possible once human praxis has created a new society. The problem is to discover the basic structure of this praxis. History is continuously making itself through men who are neither the playthings of the circumstances and situations in which they find themselves, nor the instruments of a determinism that implies an unavoidable finality. Men are both subjects and objects, and knowledge, even supposedly scientific Marxist knowledge, involves subjectivity. Marx himself insisted upon this. 'The main defect of past materialism is that the object, reality, the world of the senses, are looked upon only as *objects* or as intuitions, but not as concrete human activity, as practical things and in a subjective way.' (*First thesis on Feuerbach*, quoted by Merleau-Ponty in *Sens et Non-sens*, p. 139)

The *Critique de la Raison Dialectique* is not a philosophy of history but an attempt to reconcile the views expressed in *L'Etre et le Néant* with Marxism, and by so doing, to see how the individual can break out of his isolation and develop a certain consciousness of co-existence, and look upon his individual conscience not as pure nihilating freedom but as freedom reflecting and being reflected by other freedoms, whose existence implies the consciousness of being an integral part of historical forces that call forth the action or rather the praxis that will, in the end, liberate man. This entails the acceptance, by the social unit that Sartre describes as the group-in-fusion, of conflict and violence as a dialectic of collective growth, bent upon embracing the totality of history. This last work of Sartre is more laboured than *L'Etre et le Néant*, and its involved examples of what he calls the 'practico-inert', together with his conversion of praxis into anti-praxis through alienated objectification, are difficult to follow. His attempts to avoid Cartesian dualism and to achieve a monism of matter are unsuccessful, for if man is mediated by things, it is only in as far as things are mediated by man, therefore, up to a point, man remains, as Protagoras put it, the measure of all things, but this measure is no longer a monadic subjectivity, cleft into an in-itself and a for-itself, but a consciousness which is an integral part of existence in situation and involved in the making of history.

Existentialism is, as previously mentioned, a literary as well as a philosophical activity. Sartre's drama, which is the primary cause of his world-wide fame and is as important as his philosophical work, undeniably reaches a high level of achievement, and places him among the half-dozen great dramatists of our time. In fact, Sartre would have liked to devote himself to art, but he realised that the subtle metaphysical ideas with which he was possessed could not be properly expounded or explained in purely literary works, so that he was practically compelled to duplicate each of them with a philosophical essay.

Le Diable et le Bon Dieu (1951), it seems to me, is a great play, on a level with the best of Brecht, Claudel or Eugene O'Neill. *Le Diable et le Bon Dieu* fits into the category of the great epic tragedies, like *Mother Courage, Galileo, Le Soulier de Satin* and *The Iceman Cometh.* Its main theme is good and evil, and man's incapacity to play at being God and to do only good on earth. This is not possible, for even his best intentions are necessarily stained with evil, and he must accept his fallen, finite state, and walk in humility the path of the saint, as is the case with Rodrigue in *Le Soulier de Satin*, or repudiate the absent or uncomprehending God and perform unflinchingly the task he has been born for, even if, as in the case of Goetz, this task consists in continuous fighting and killing. Encouraged by the eternal serpent, in the shape of an evil priest, Goetz gives up his lands to the poor at the wrong moment, at a moment when the poor do not so much need land to work on as a good general to lead them. The result of this move is disaster. The hastily built new Jerusalem is destroyed under the very eyes of Goetz who, caught in the dilemma of being unable to do good except through bloodshed, refuses to act and allows the peasants to be slaughtered, while he retires from the world and devotes himself to love. He appeals in vain to God to show him the way and to destroy what is foul in him; God remains silent, while Heinrich, the evil priest, informs him that the peasants have been destroyed and that he, Goetz, is merely an impostor. Goetz sees the light and realises that his attempt to raise himself to God's level and to challenge Him as an equal to acknowledge him so as to prove His existence, has failed. He has failed because 'there is no God, God is the loneliness of man. . . . I alone decided on evil, I alone invented God, . . .I have delivered us, no more Heaven, no more

Hell; nothing but earth. . . . Men are born criminals, I must demand my share of their crimes if I want my share of their love. . . . I wanted only pure love. Sheer nonsense. . . . On this earth at this time good and evil are inseparable. I accept my share of evil to inherit my share of good.' (*Le Diable et le Bon Dieu*, p. 133 *et seq.*)

If no other play of Sartre reaches the height of *Le Diable et le Bon Dieu*, *Les Séquestrés de l'Altona*, *Les Mains Sales* and *Huis Clos* are nevertheless among the best plays of our time. They are tense, perfectly orchestrated dramatic constructions sustained by characters that are deeply moving and express wide areas of human affectivity. *Les Séquestrés de l'Altona* (1960), a very complex drama with various layers of meaning, is a model of what a drama that aims at revealing the conflicting forces of society at a given moment should be. There are no cardboard characters or allegories to be unravelled by Byzantine minds. Sartre's deep political experience and maturity of thought together with his burning concern about injustice, individual or national guilt, are made to come to life through a cluster of people, interrelated, interlocked in love-hate complexes which luminously mirror other conflicts, other complexes that can be solved only by death, making possible new births. We do not have here the transparency of O'Neill's masterpieces, simply because Sartre's temperament carries with it a certain turgidity, a philosophical urge to relate men to ideas and pressures that are dear to him and that unavoidably impinge on the dramatist as dramatist; yet, the pressure of ideology is minimal, and the play is a profound and enriching experience whose characters and the situations which they embody will mirror, for ages to come, a living aspect of the tragic plight of twentieth-century man. His main character Franz, and through him Germany and the world, are shown to be guilt-ridden, locked in the past, harrowed by memories of inhuman tortures, in which both the torturers and their victims image the plight of man who cannot avoid causing suffering, and suffering from what he has done, for, contrary to what Sartre has said in *Les Mouches*, conscience pursues him and constantly reminds him of the fact that evil is inherent in man: remorse is the crab which constantly feeds upon his heart. Franz has to be justified, to be liberated by a presence, a gaze outside himself, for the other here is not what destroys, but what gives existence its reality. It is Johanna who does this by recognising him as the beast that he is, by conferring upon him a true reality that only death can abolish. Here we have gone beyond *Huis Clos*, with human beings truly in situation in the world, and not merely frozen as essences in the consciousness of others. The deaths of Franz and his father are as real as the death of the guilty part of Germany or of any nation or group of people who have practised torture. These rotten aspects of man will have to die, so that a new humanity may arise.

This is the conclusion of Sartre's journey from a solipsistic, partially idealistic philosophy to a philosophy of action and existence involved in historical time. It is a philosophy that Sartre has not only practised but expressed in numerous essays collected in ten volumes entitled *Situations*, which show the breadth of his knowledge and interests, and the mastery of his skill as a writer, nowhere better illustrated than in *La Nausée* or in his short autobiographical work *Les Mots* which confirms the fact that Sartre is the most versatile literary genius of our time and, with Heidegger, the greatest living thinker.

6

Religious Existentialism

Gabriel Marcel, Louis Lavelle, Jacques Maritain

The contemporary form of existentialism is due, above all, to
Sartre who has propounded an atheistic existentialism, but the
fact remains that the basically religious foundation of existentialism has survived Sartre's unsatisfactory attempts to dispose of it,
and that existentialism is bound to remain, first and foremost,
connected with transcendental notions which atheism seeks to
repudiate. The incarnation as the crux of the Christian religion
brings the *logos* into existence and stresses the importance of
existence as informed with being, part of Being. From St
Augustine to Pascal—who, as a Jansenist, was basically
Augustinian, obsessed by the sense of sin and the need for
gratuitous, unpredictable grace, and prepared the way for
Kierkegaard and for contemporary existentialism—a philosophy
of being based on being in the world, part of the world, was one
of the basic strands of human thought and was bound, at some
time or another, to emerge as the dominant one, as an answer
to discarded idealism and absolute rationalism. Pascal's awareness of the incapacity of man's reason to grasp the workings of
God's mind or the mystery of Being, underlies the need to accept
the irrational as a necessary part of life and of the finitude of
man. Reason as the absolute cannot be comprehended; Kant
accepted this limitation, and knowing has never been equated
with believing, for certainty is not necessarily truth. But there
is a certainty of experience, and a truth of experience which,
though not verifiable or falsifiable, has validity in its own domain
and makes it impossible to say that life is an absurd, useless
passion, for it is obvious that this statement is not a truth but
merely a subjective pronouncement, as irrational as the absurdity
it ascribes to the world.

117

The notion of the absurdity of the world, propounded by a necessarily absurd existent who is part of it, is as contradictory as the notion that leads Camus to conclude his attempt to describe the absurd in *The Myth of Sisyphus* with the words : 'We must suppose Sisyphus happy.' This conclusion fails to take into account the fact that we can suppose Sisyphus happy only by having him reconciled with a form of rationality or order that he does not understand, because it is beyond him, but that he nevertheless accepts in the name of a kind of human stoicism and nobility that enables him to transcend his fate. By so doing, he posits values that necessarily destroy the absurdity of the world, for whether God-made or man-made, values must be rational and universal, and Sisyphus's apparently hopeless, absurd task thus becomes an ethical *ought to*, a duty that enables him, as a man, to display his moral nobility and greatness. These two values are enough to make life worth while and to wash away from it any notion of absurdity. Though it is not Sisyphus himself who is asked to declare himself happy—something that would imply a reconciliation to his task and his acceptance of rationality in the universe—his fellow beings are asked to do so for him, and that is, in fact, the same thing, for his fellow beings are part of the same world to which he belongs, and man or human consciousness is unthinkable without a *thou*, without the other. Even Christ said : 'For where two or three are gathered together in my name, there am I in the midst of them.' He did not say : 'I am with you alone.' And Heidegger, an atheistic existentialist, said : 'The world is what I share with others.' (*Sein und Zeit*, Niemeyer Verlag, Tübingen, 1927, p. 117)

Man is man in situation in the world. This reflection brings me to the question of subjectivity, which is the basis of existentialism. 'Subjectivity is truth; . . . I do not know truth except when it becomes life in me. . . . Freedom consists precisely in that bold venture that chooses objective incertitude with the passion of the infinite.' Thus Kierkegaard, the modern archetype of existentialism. Hegel, at least the later Hegel, had reached the conclusion that the rational is the real; for Kierkegaard, life is anything but rational, and any attempt to prove the existence of God is blasphemy and a destruction of faith, for faith must be chosen or opted for, because it is not rational but paradoxical, because, as Marcel sees it, it is part of the mystery of being. To believe, one must start not from dogmas or revelation, but from oneself in situation, oneself as a body in the world, a body which must be assumed as a centre of uncertainties. Yet, my body carries one absolute, non-Cartesian certainty—that of existence, which is revealed to me through my subjectivity. I am aware of my body, therefore I am; but this awareness, this subjectivity, necessarily extends beyond the awareness of oneself; it extends to other selves, and it becomes the transcendental intersubjectivity or substratum of Being to which all subjectivities can, in the requisite conditions, have access and through which they achieve an awareness of existence which is also awareness of freedom, for freedom can consist only in being aware of one's own true being as perfectly attuned with the plenitude of Being.

Existence can neither be the source nor the end of subjectivity which transcends it through the absolute of intersubjectivity. The absolute is the inner totality which individuated subjectivities endeavour to reach and merge into, but can never fully achieve in existence. The absolute is the source and finality of pure subjectivity which is separated from it by existence. One must not therefore confuse existential subjectivity and the absolute. Reason must keep in mind the fact that in existence this absolute is not subjectivity, for it is separated from it by subjectivity's finitude.

Gabriel Marcel

Although he has not achieved the fame of Sartre or of Merleau-Ponty, Gabriel Marcel (1889–1973) is a very important philosopher to whom both Sartre and Merleau-Ponty owe far more than is generally acknowledged. One must not forget the fact that Marcel published his famous *Metaphysical Journal* the very year that Heidegger published *Sein und Zeit*, in 1927, and five years before Bergson's *Les Deux Sources de la Morale et de la Religion*. The *Metaphysical Journal* contains many of the notions that have become by now the stock-in-trade of existentialism, and whose originality has been obfuscated by the fame of those who have popularised existentialism. The notion of being in situation, the importance of the body as a centre of connections with the world, and the refusal to start from abstractions and systems, are basic to Marcel's thought. Marcel denied having what is called a philosophy, and he would confess that nothing startled him more than the kind of question often put to him at the end of a lecture: What is your philosophy? He has no philosophy; he is looking for one, and that is, according to him, the task of the philosopher, for 'philosophy is experience, a way of knowing and apprehending oneself'. (*Du Refus à l'Invocation*, Gallimard, 1940, p. 25) The object of his search is not the foundation of a system, or a means of expounding his view of the world, but a certain type of wisdom obtained through experience, and through deeper and deeper explorations into the inner self. Such searches and explorations can, according to Marcel, best be carried out through the situations and tensions of drama, through the anguish of lived experience, and through the serenity and detachment provided by music. These three different domains of exploration exclude systematic rationalisations and abstractions. Marcel is, in this respect, thoroughly Bergsonian; his aim is 'to restore the concrete beyond the disjointed deductions and fragmentations of abstract thought.' (*Ibid.*, p. 34) That is why he has repeated time and time again that his theatre, regrettably neglected because it does not correspond to the fashion of the day, is an integral part of his philosophy, and is a way of discovering or of recovering the truth he is looking for. 'My philosophy is not separate from my theatre which is not an illustration or a translation of abstract thought into concrete terms. . . . In truth one must give pre-eminence to my theatre.'* (*Présence et Immortalité*, Flammarion, 1959, p. 13)

Philosophy is a form of hope and a journey towards truth, a journey never completed, interrupted only by death. In that respect Marcel rejoins Merleau-Ponty, and like him he starts from the senses and from perceptions in search of the mystery of being. What is being? And the first and vital answer to this question is that: 'We cannot question ourselves about being

* Having been a devoted friend of Gabriel Marcel for a very long time, it is sad for me to say that though I admire some of his plays, I find that on the whole their subtle and profound dialogue is not matched by the kind of striking situations and structures that could have made of some of them first-rate drama.

as if the questioning subject were out of being.' (*Fragments Philosophiques*, Nauwelaerts, 1964, p. 45) This is a basic fact which precludes abstractions and examinations of being as object. Marcel believes that : 'There is a mystery in the act of knowing; knowledge is bound up with the mode of participation, which no epistemology can account for, because it implies this participation.' (*Position et Approches du Mystère Ontologique*, Nauwelaerts and Vrin, 1945, p. 57) So that as far as knowledge of being is concerned, there are limits beyond which one cannot go. Truth is that towards which we progress, and it is also that which urges us on in our progression; it is therefore both our aim and a kind of presence of a force that compels us towards this aim. At the end of this progression there is an encounter between what we were searching for and what in us enables us to recognise what we were looking for; there is therefore a recognition of what we carried in us in what we pursued. Truth is both in us and outside us, and our aim is to connect both aspects of ourselves as part of true being.

For Marcel, 'to exist is to coexist'. (*Présence et Immortalité*, p. 162) This is clearly opposed to Sartre's view that the for-itself does not entail any form of participation. Marcel dealt well before Sartre with the problem of bad faith involved in accusing others of defects we are not supposed to have. 'To exist, for an individual consciousness, is to be in relationship with others.' (*Journal Métaphysique*, Gallimard, 1927, p. 235) 'Joy is nothing but acting in communion with the totality of being.' (*Ibid.*, p. 230) Faith is accession to or union with true reality, and transcendence means the acknowledgement of the existence of a primal bond which unites all men, and this bond is the existence of a divine Father. The encounter with God is the encounter with a presence that is the principle of the whole intersubjectivity; 'God is invoked by myself and becomes the absolute thou.' (*Ibid.*, p. 287) Marcel's philosophy is not a Christian philosophy, if one means by that a philosophy that derives its basic concepts and orientations from a given theology. Philosophy for him is 'a commitment based upon a presentiment'. (*Présence et Immortalité*, p. 136) It is a search for being accepted as mystery, therefore not rationally knowable, but apprehensible as participation in the intersubjective nature of love which is joy and light. For Marcel, God and creation form a vast symphony in which all—the living and the dead—play a part, each according to his own vocation.

For Marcel, morality or ethics always starts from the concrete, from a human being who finds himself in a given situation. His method is Socratic; it is a kind of maieutic, and he himself describes his philosophy as neo-Socratism. He has time and again repudiated the title of Christian existentialist, a title that would make it appear as if the only difference between him and Sartre were the belief in the existence or non-existence of God.* That would be an over-simplification, for it might lead one to think that Marcel bases his morality upon the existence of an absolute, or of essences or ideas, to which existence conforms. That would be wrong, for Marcel always starts from being in situation, and it is from this situation that man has to work for or against being, for 'the principle of what we call value can only be being. . . . Value is a kind of refraction of being.' (*Les Hommes contre l'Humain*, La Colombe, 1951, p. 122) 'These values appear as answers to a kind of call, which generally becomes conscious of itself only in as far as the answer becomes clear.' (*Ibid.*, p. 128) This call can be based only on love, part of being. 'Love is not a value, but there cannot be any value without love.' (*Ibid.*, p. 140)

The universality of values rests upon the universality of being; values are universal as refractions of being, and as refractions they are necessarily limited because of the existent's partial lack of being. This form of thinking, whose connections with aspects of Platonism are evident, rejoins at the same time aspects of Christian thought that look upon creation as implying a necessary withdrawal of Being, and also aspects of atheistic existentialism that look upon existence as implying a lack of being. It seems that, wherever it may turn, the human mind, in various ways, always equates existence and finitude with a certain lack of being, or with a certain negativity which makes existence

---

* He refused to be defined as a Christian existentialist in the same way as T. S. Eliot refused to be defined as a Christian poet and both François Mauriac and Graham Greene have refused to be defined as Christian or Catholic novelists.

possible. The mention of the word 'Platonism' should ꝼ
rise to any misleading conclusion. For Marcel, as well
Sartre or Heidegger, man is not determined, but detei
what he himself will be; but the difference in the case of Marcel
is that man realises himself not through gratuitous choices in a
meaningless world, but as an existent intent upon transcending
himself in answer to aspirations towards a Being, of which he is
part and which he will partially know once he has reached
certain states of detachment or achieved the ascent towards it,
which is man's true destiny.

This brings us to the much discussed question of freedom—a
practically intractable concept, except as part and parcel of well
delineated fields of action or thought. It is evident that the
notion of freedom has nothing to do with the notion of doing
whatever one likes, for in such a sense no one is free, not even
God. Nor is freedom the indefinable product of Kant's pure
reason. Is then freedom the total independence or liberation from
desires? Or is it the Sartrian pure power of choice, 'the nothingness that inserts itself between motives and actions'? (*L'Etre et
le Néant*, p. 71) But nothingness is nothingness, therefore there
is nothing inserted between the motives and the actions, and so
motives and actions are one, or rather action is all, without any
basic dividing line between good and evil, without any *a priori*
notion of value by which to judge action. For Sartre action or
choice is in itself a value that is good, and as man is condemned
to freedom, he cannot but choose, and he does not have to worry
as to what he chooses, in fact the choice makes itself, for it is
based on nothingness; so we have an ethics of total detachment,
and we have to be so, as Sartre put it, 'without regrets and
without remorse'. (*Ibid.*, p. 641) This is possible only in the
fictional world of *Les Mouches* in which Orestes, the hero, does
or says exactly what his creator, Sartre, tells him to do or say,
but it requires more than a suspension of belief or disbelief to
allow oneself to confer any human reality on this character, who
is less alive in his philosophical lack of coherence than any one
of the characters of Plato's philosophical dialogues.

Marcel's views are different. For him, 'to say that I am free
means that I am myself'. (*Le Mystère de l'Etre*, Aubier, 1951,
p. 115) Freedom is the articulation of individual existence upon

being, and therefore of existence itself upon being. It is a participation in being, and the scope and range of this participation are determined by our capacity or incapacity to love. Every human being is aware that the essence of his existence is a gratuitous gift which he receives and must use in accordance with this basic notion of life as gift. Therefore the more and the better one gives, the more one receives, and human freedom is for Marcel what it is for true Christians, the power to apprehend the grace or the gift of being. We are the more free as we are open to Being which transcends us. We are back to Dante's words : 'In la sua voluntade e nostra pace.' Freedom is the awareness of our true, authentic being. It is the end of an interior journey which leads us to our sources, to what we truly are, to the point where the subject ceases being purely himself, and connects with the intersubjectivity which enables him to be aware that he is both himself and part of a transcendental self or universal intersubjectivity. This is, it seems to me, the only concept of freedom that is rational and avoids impossible divisions between self and will, and self and virtualities of action or choices that are non-existent, and consequently non-knowable, until they are realised. Therefore, their realisation is not due to will preceded by choice, but to intuitive decisions, which are more or less part of being—more if they favour the plenitude of being, less if they work towards the diminution or the denial of being.

Freedom, says Marcel, is our true authentic being, and the non-authentic is for him, as for Heidegger, oblivious of being and of Being. Man, by recognising his dependence upon Being, recognises also his fraternity with other men, and it is this fraternity that makes him a participant in the universal. Authenticity, for Marcel, is participation in being; for Sartre, it is refusal of bad faith, but this bad faith is, as we have seen, extremely difficult to define, for it is most of the time the other who decides for us what bad faith is. Thus Sartre decides for Baudelaire and Flaubert, and he does so as part of a philosophy that looks upon the other as the enemy, who diminishes us and causes hell for us. For Marcel, the other enriches us, because he is not an enemy but a brother, because human dignity is authentic freedom, and because love, which is the motive of the search for true being, can only make us look upon the other as a brotherly 'thou'. The good is the call from Being, a call which men hear according to their capacity to listen and their desire to contribute to the fulfilment of Being in creation. Evil is a refusal of Being, and the objectification of the individual self as a self-caused, self-fulfilling entity—an entity that ignores or denies any essential connection with other selves or with Being. It is this attitude that makes violence, wars and atrocities possible. If man is looked upon not as a brother, but as object, called a Jew, a German, a Vietcong, a Communist, a Fascist or whatever one likes, then the death or violence inflicted upon him is not real and therefore not shared by the one who inflicts it, and who will go on inflicting it until men look upon one another as men.

Evil and suffering are real; they are not notions that can easily be disposed of by any Leibnizian vision of transcendental harmony. They are undeniably part of the life of the individual self condemned to suffer because of its limitations, and condemned to death because of its finitude; but the end of man, says Marcel, is beyond death, and the philosopher must search for truth and push to the extreme the will to communicate. This communication or communion must pass through the depth of the self, through explorations of individual consciousness, and be integrated into love in search for Being. One must realise that truth is not a possession (*un avoir*), truth is participation in being, but is not identical with Being, for Being is incommensurable. The transcendence of truth or of freedom is the transcendence of being, and this being remains mysterious, as mysterious as Being or God, with whom man is connected. And Marcel not only accepts this mystery, but in fact finds it necessary to the nature of his belief in God. 'The only God in which I can believe is a God Who accepts, in a certain sense, that it should be possible to doubt Him.' (*Présence et Immortalité*, p. 92) He may doubt Him, but he does not doubt His fatherhood of men, and this fatherhood is absolutely necessary to the notion of human fraternity and to the hope for living, for we only rise to authentic life through hope. 'I am inclined to believe that hope is to the soul what breathing is to living being; wherever hope is lacking, the soul wilts and perishes.' (*Homo Viator*, Aubier, 1945, p. 10)

Louis Lavelle

Like Bergson and Merleau-Ponty, Louis Lavelle (1883–1951) held the chair of philosophy at the Collège de France. His philosophy is a philosophy of Being. For him Being is experienced by an individual act of consciousness as an act of communion or an act of faith. The word 'act' has here its full meaning of action; Being itself is pure Act, self-caused, continuously creating itself as it continuously sustains existence. 'The world endlessly begins at every instant.' (*De l'Acte*, Aubier, 1937, p. 112) Existence is continuous participation in the pure Act, and Lavelle's philosophy has been truly described as a philosophy of participation. Everything that exists partakes of Being, which sustains the existence of all things. But this participation in Being is not simply real existence. The pure Act alone really exists, not only through its own agency, by being its own causation, but also in itself. 'It is only for those who look towards God that the real possesses essence; for all other men it is composed only of phenomena.' (*Ibid.*, p. 107) This is the pure Platonism that was absorbed into Christianity in the form of Augustinianism. With the notion that being has to be constantly sustained as a grace or a gift from God or Being, we pass from Augustinianism to Jansenism and, up to a point, to Calvinism. Anyway, this is a notion absolutely central to the Christian faith. Without Being or God, there would be no possibilities of existence, and the word 'possibilities' is important because it makes it clear that although Being is necessary to existence, it does not determine all the aspects of existence : 'Being can bring into existence only beings that are called upon to make themselves.' (*La Présence Totale*, Aubier, 1934, p. 16)

For Lavelle men make themselves, as for Marcel or Merleau-Ponty, with their body which is both matter and spirit welded into a unity which defies dualism but which, as far as existence on earth is concerned, remains an appearance and a means of attaining true life or death. Man is a being engaged in matter or in time which separates him from Being, and he must, through time, bridge this gap or widen it. He does so through his spirit or consciousness which is not an epiphenomenon of the body, but an integral part of it, and a means without which man's awareness of the universe and of his fellow beings would not be possible. Man is therefore part of the material universe and he rises to participation in the creativity of the pure Act through spirit, which enables him to conceive of the universal and to transcend the limitations of his individuation and finitude, which are the gap or interval that separate him from the pure Act or transcendence. This spatio-temporal terminology is not appropriate in this context, for it is evident that Being and being are not separated by time or space, but are part of an existential terminology which, operating from finitude, sees being as separated from Being, something that from the point of view of Being is not, and cannot be, the case. We shall return to this point later, with the problem of time.

Long before Sartre, Lavelle had expounded the basic tenets of existentialism. 'To exist is to posit oneself or to have the possibility of positing onself, that is to say to be able to acquire essence' (*De l'Acte*, p. 102); and further : 'existence is only given to man for the express purpose of achieving essence.' (*Ibid.*, p. 103) But the essence here acquired is not the Sartrian essence, the ashes of a burnt-out life, what is left from an existence, what the others think that this existence truly has been, but on the contrary the essence that connects with Being, and therefore decides the degree of participation of an individuated being in Being. What one has been in life decides what one will be in God or in the pure Act. This is a very Christian thought, in the sense that it is in existence that we decide what our essence or capacity for eternity will be, once this essence has been refined through actualisation. 'Existence has no other meaning except to permit us, not to realise an essence, but to determine it by our choice and to identify ourselves with it. . . . It is by the choice of our essence that we establish our eternal place in Being.' (*Ibid.*, p. 95) This is done by participating freely in the act of the Creator, and consciousness consists in the awareness of this participation. This is in fact a very orthodox Christian point of view, which consists in resting man's awareness of existence on his awareness of his connection with God or Being, in moments of grace. To think, says Lavelle, is to be conscious of oneself in participation with being, and to know oneself is to create oneself.

To know is to be born with, or to be born again, said Claudel. Thus through repeated acts of consciousness as awareness of being, man creates himself as God creates the world. The individual self for Lavelle knows itself only by expressing itself, and it expresses itself by realising the plenitude of the potentialities latent in itself.

Man's freedom cannot be absolute, for man cannot avoid positing himself in situation in the world as an existent, part of being, therefore informed with certain possibilities and limitations. He starts from the world in a material body, and it is from the position of body-spirit in the world or in existence that he can raise himself to his true being. This cannot be done without effort, attention and concentration upon essentials, in order to discover the true self. This search goes on throughout life, and 'we are never entirely present to ourselves until the moment of our death'. (*La Conscience de Soi*, Grasset, 1933, p. 258) The life of the self is essentially project, pursuit of an ideal or a design to be achieved, in order to reach fulfilment. The awareness of the existence of this constant guiding light implies the existence of norms, of values that have nothing to do with Sartrian existentialism and constant creation of value through choice.

But if Lavelle differs from Sartre in many respects, he shares with him the sense of risk implied by choice and arbitrary decisions. Like Sartre, he feels that the individual assumes not only his destiny but that of others. 'I am in a certain sense responsible for what you think and do.' (*L'Erreur de Narcisse*, Grasset, 1939, p. 68) But this responsibility is obviously limited by the individual's capacities which depend both on his essence and on Being with which essence is connected. 'All that we have done has consequences here and in eternity, which are not for us to foresee or fear, for they are not the result of our will but of the ordering of the world.' (*Ibid.*, p. 188) We are no doubt back to Christian thought, but whether with Pascal, Kierkegaard or Marcel, Christian thought does not exclude anxiety and despair, and Lavelle describes this particular anguish as 'expressing no more than the supreme tension of its hope'. (*La Présence Totale*, p. 10) Lavelle is what could be called an essentialist existentialist; his Penelope, like Whitehead's, like that of most great philosophers of the Western world, is Plato. 'One is a philosopher in as far as one thinks in Plato's terms,' he says. God for him is the Being in which essence and existence are one and which embraces all the possibilities and virtualities of existence. Essence therefore precedes existence in time and informs it and is greatly responsible for its finality. This is the world of Thomas Aquinas, with its notions of an ideal human nature and a rationality to which the individual endeavours to conform. The choice of the individual is therefore limited by his essence and by his nature. An individuated being is the result of an individuation of essence that carries possibilities and virtualities from which emerges what is necessary for the full realisation of himself. The problem is to discover the true essence, for by itself existence is valueless; 'it is essence that confers value upon it.' (*De l'Acte*, p. 101) It is the value of what is chosen that gives value to the choice, but the choice is not a value in itself.

For Lavelle, as for Plato, the sensible world is no more than a shadow of the real world; and the world of ideas, though it blinds us, also guides us. 'The real world is the world of ideas and not that of things, and the world gives us the norms of our values and tells us what conduct we must follow and what relations we must have with our fellow beings. We do not create ideas. They are the elements of the universe of thought. . . . They reveal themselves to us through attention.' (*La Conscience de Soi*, p. 60) In order to compose our spiritual self, or our true self, we must choose from among these ideas the ones that we require so as to be ourselves. 'It is possible to say that all ideas come from God; but the order in which they are organised belongs to man.' (*Ibid.*, p. 61) There seems to be here an equation between ideas and virtualities and possibilities of existence that is not tenable. There are no grounds for equating the infinite possibilities of life, the material from which existence and actualisations emerge, with the ideas which, as structures of the mind, correspond to, or crystallise in themselves, vast stretches of the patterns of human thought that are also the structural patterns of nature.

For Lavelle, man makes himself, but he chooses out of ideals and norms that are part of the possibilities of existence. The aim of this choice is to achieve participation in Being. Time is the gap between the totality of Being and individual being; it is the awareness perceived by individual consciousness of the lack of being so as to be part of the totality of Being; it is therefore the awareness of a partial absence of being which must be redeemed through time, so that time might be forever abolished. Freedom, which is awareness of being, is also awareness of non-temporality, that is to say of timelessness. Time is, as with Plato, the becoming or duration of Eternity, as a means of refining, through existence, the pure being that belongs to Eternity. Eternity makes itself in time, and through time. Lavelle endeavours to reconcile a free spiritual activity with the existence of a Being which, through essence, informs existence. The finitude of the individual self is the gap that separates it from God or Being; it is this gap that makes it possible for the being in time to prepare its final place in the whole or totality of Being.

The existence of Being cannot, of course, be proved, but the task of rationality, which is an inherent part of Being, is to justify faith in its existence and not to destroy this faith. God or Being is pure Act, and the individuated self endeavours to participate in this pure Act, but the world or time is the gap that stands in the way of this participation, and therefore the world or time has to be used to make this participation possible. In order to do that, the individuated self must not commit the error of turning its gaze inwards into itself, that is to say to its own egoism and self-interest. If the self does that, it commits Narcissus' error, seeking the adoration of its own image and then drowning itself in its own egoism. The individuated self must search for its true self, or true being, and thus discover the universal, the intersubjectivity, in which all true selves are reunited. This is also Marcel's inward journey, and that of most Christian mystics.

The search for the true self must avoid being sidetracked into vain superficial pursuit. Man is what he is essentially only when addressed by Being, said Heidegger, and in order that he might be addressed by Being he must be in a state of pure receptivity or openness which can be obtained only by the abolition of the self, as is the case with mysticism. We truly exist only if we are sincere with ourselves, in accord with our true self, an authentic expression of it. In order to do that, we must endeavour to discover our true essence. This is not easy, for essence cannot be objectified, cannot be known except through its existential manifestations; therefore its discovery is a matter of discipline, of action, of doing certain things, of bringing into play certain attitudes and feelings that are part of the true self, and therefore of being. This search for the true self is a kind of shedding of egotistical impediments, preoccupations with the dark aspects of life, with evil, with the forces that divide men. It is a search for the good, for serenity, wisdom and joy, in the certainty that the divine Presence which informs creation is intent upon individual participation in this continuously creative act which is an act of love. Time and Eternity are coeval; time is necessary to Being, for without it, Being would remain an eternal field of possibilities and virtualities, unsieved by existence. Without Being, being would be pure contingence; as the becoming of Being, it is the duration that makes possible the participation of being in the pure Act, and therefore in Eternity.

The most distinctive trait of Lavelle's philosophy is that it brings about a synthesis between existentialism and essentialism or Platonism as interpreted by St Augustine. For Lavelle, as for Plato, the sensible world is only a shadow of the real world which is the world of ideas. 'We do not in any sense create ideas. They are part of the universe of thought, as solid things are part of the universe. They reveal themselves to us through an act of attention. . . . Our pure activity chooses from among the ideas, and by the way it assembles them it composes our spiritual person. . . . All ideas come from God.' (*La Conscience de Soi*, pp. 60–61) For Lavelle, we choose our true self or person through our actions, but we choose from ideas and ideals that are part of the Eternal world or of God. We make ourselves both in time and in Eternity, out of infinite possibilities from which we choose; we make ourselves as part of an eternal world, and also for an eternal world.

Jacques Maritain

Pope Paul described Jacques Maritain (1882–1973) as the greatest theologian of our time. This is both an adequate assessment of Maritain's place and importance in contemporary thought, and also an explanation as to the reason why, in spite of the wide range of his philosophical work, he does not enjoy the reputation or influence that ought to flow from it. He is, certainly, highly respected in the Catholic Church, though not without some protests from those who find his thinking and his attitude towards certain problems too uncompromising and too radical. But he is largely ignored by students and philosophers who are much preoccupied with linguistics, with subjective thought and sensibility, and with pure intellectualism. Maritain is not, generally, described as an existentialist, yet he is a disciple or a commentator of Thomas Aquinas, and like Thomas Aquinas, he is not only concerned with the rationality of creation, he is also deeply concerned with existence and being, and with the importance of Time as informed with God's presence. Like Aquinas, he is a critical realist. His existentialism is an objective rationalism of the kind that was displaced by Hegel's idealism and, faith apart, was only partly reinstated by Marx.

Maritain reunites realism* and metaphysics, and reasserts, with Aristotle and with Thomas Aquinas, the importance of intelligence, of objectivity and the human concern with the real. Thomas Aquinas put an end to Augustinian Platonism. He marks the transition from the cult of the intelligible forms of Augustinian neo-Platonism, of abstractions and geometrical shapes and idealised beauty and knowledge through God or the One, to experimental knowledge, rationality, acceptance of experience in art and life, and to the vital importance of existence and reality in time. With Aquinas we pass from geometrical Norman art to Gothic congruence with all aspects of reality, and above all with rational observation and experience. Faith in science and observation did not wait for Descartes; it began with Aquinas in the wake of Aristotle.

Maritain belongs to this world. He is concerned with being, with God's activity in the world, through man as a rational being, and not as a fragment of flotsam adrift in a world born by chance and without causes or finality. It is because of his

---

* The theory that objects or matter have real existence independently of any perceiver. For a Christian, the real world—God-created—is informed with God's subsistent essence.

rational search for the absolute, in a world that repudiates the absolute and is intent upon deconstruction or destruction, that Maritain is, alas, ignored. The intelligentsia, the French more than any other, is fighting on against types of values that have been destroyed long ago, through the evolution of science and society. These were bourgeois, naturalistic values that died largely with the nineteenth century and finally with the First World War. Yet, the proletariat in all its forms, undeniably the rising force, the ruling force of tomorrow, does not and cannot recognise its psyche in abstract art or linguistic acrobatics. It is concerned with reality, and therefore, whether in Marxism or in Maritain's Christian realism, that is where the answer to the questions of tomorrow's society lies.

If Maritain has not yet met his deserved success as a philosopher, he has certainly made a deep mark with his views on art. His books *Art et Scolastique* (1920) and *Creative Intuition in Art and Poetry* (1953) show that, both at a first-hand level and thanks to the help of his wife Raissa who was a poet, he was able to achieve a grasp of the process of artistic creation that places his name by the side of those of Croce, Collingwood or Worringer. As for his philosophy of being, best summed up in his important books like *Distinguer pour Unir, ou les Degrés du Savoir* (1932) and *Eléments de Philosophie* (1920–23), it could find its true place only if the world became more aware that it has to look upon reality and being as the primary concerns of man. The *Times Literary Supplement* of 5 April 1974 (p. 374) made a comment which can be appropriately quoted here : 'It is many years since T. S. Eliot hailed Jacques Maritain as the "most important influence in contemporary French philosophy". This was a slight, though pardonable, exaggeration in the lifetime of Bergson and Blondel. . . .' No doubt it was, and it is all the more so today when Maritain's theological explorations and his deep moral concern do not command much response from our society.

7

Albert Camus

Albert Camus (1913–60) was not a philosopher, or to be precise a thinker, who was able to express a coherent view of man's relation to his fellow beings and to the society and the time in which he was living. His two philosophical essays, *Le Mythe de Sisyphe* (1942) and *L'Homme Révolté* (1951), are not philosophically coherent, and it would not be very fruitful to submit them to a critical examination. As far as *L'Homme Révolté* is concerned, this has already been brilliantly done by Sartre, who, it must be conceded, was perfectly sound in his devastating philosophical conclusions. Yet, though Camus is not a philosopher, his name and his work are so deeply associated with existentialism and with the notion of the absurd which is part of it, that it would be unthinkable and inappropriate not to say a few words about him, even although this survey of twentieth-century French thought lays no claim to being an exhaustive study of the subject. If Camus' philosophical status and importance are minimal, his importance as a novelist and as a moralist, even in the heyday of existentialism, has been second only to that of Sartre, and might even be ahead of it now. That is why something must be said about the philosophical ideas and attitudes that remain associated with his name. Besides, one may not praise his philosophical coherence and skill, but one cannot but deeply admire his undeniable concern for man, his sincerity, generosity, and humanism, admirably expressed in novels like *La Peste*, *L'Etranger* or *La Chute*, which are accomplished enough to have won him an important place in contemporary literature.

I cannot confess any real enthusiasm for his theatre, not even for *Caligula*, and this in spite of the fact that, like Gabriel

Marcel, he was deeply attached to it, and that as a producer and actor he was truly a man of the theatre. What must be praised without any possible reservations are his marvellous adaptations of Dostoyevsky's *The Possessed*, William Faulkner's *Requiem for a Nun*, Lope de Vega's *Le Chevalier d'Olmeda*, and, of course, his memorable essays, *L'Exil et le Royaume*, *L'Eté*, *L'Envers et l'Endroit*, *Noces*, *Lettre à un Ami allemand*, etc., to say nothing of his voluminous journalistic contributions which showed a tormented concern for human problems and situations which no easy, clear-cut dogmatism could solve. All these works demonstrate Camus' mastery of style, poetic vision and psychological insight, and having known and deeply respected the man's sincerity and honesty, I should not like to have my lack of enthusiasm for his philosophical works interpreted as a lack of admiration for the outstanding writer that he was. In fact, in spite of all the mental subtleties of our modern stylists or skilful constructivists in structuralist writing, or in the domain of what is called the *nouveau roman*, Camus' achievement as a novelist remains, in my view, unsurpassed by any writer who has come after him.

This being said, let us briefly return to our topic which is philosophy. Sartre called Camus the Descartes of the absurd, and this is indeed what Camus said on that subject: 'The true characteristic of the absurd is to be a starting point, the equivalent in existence of Descartes' methodical doubt.' (*L'Homme Révolté*, Gallimard, 1951, p. 19) 'In the daily trials which are our lot, revolt plays the same role as the *cogito* in thinking. It is the first evidence, and the evidence takes man out of his solitude. It is the meeting point on which men base the first value. I revolt, therefore we are.' (*Ibid.*, p. 36) For Camus, the absurd is the basis of an ethics of solidarity and action; for Sartre, the absurd is the basis of man's loneliness and of his tragic situation: the awareness of existence does not produce an encouragement to action, but a feeling of nausea and a horror of existence. The two attitudes could not be more opposed, their ethics more contrasted. Let us explore briefly the range of Camus' notion of the absurd, which is above all associated with his name. It is, for him, neither an entity nor a quality of being, but a subjective notion concerning the relationship of man with the world and man with himself, and his confrontation with the inevitability of death. 'From this inert body upon which a slap would leave no trace, the soul has disappeared. . . . Under the mortal glare of such a destiny, uselessness stands out. No morality, no efforts can *a priori* be justified in the face of the bloody mathematics which presides over our condition.' (*Le Mythe de Sisyphe*, Gallimard, 1942, p. 30) 'Intelligence tells me, in its own way, that the world is absurd.' (*Ibid.*, p. 36) 'The feeling of the absurd does not arise from the examination, from the simple examination, of one single fact or one impression, but from the comparison between a certain situation and a certain reality, between a given action and the world which transcends it. The absurd is essentially a divorce, and it lies in neither of the two elements examined; it lies in their confrontation. . . . The absurd is neither in man . . . nor in the world . . . it lies in their common presence, it is for the moment the only bond that unites both.' (*Ibid.*, p. 48) Another quotation will complete Camus' exposition of the notion of the absurd and make clear its rather shallow aspect : 'I want to have everything explained to me or nothing. And reason remains powerless in answer to this cry of the heart, while the mind discovers only contradictions and irrationality to meet this need.' (*Ibid.*, p. 44)

Reason would like to know everything. Pascal's thinking reed, caught in anguish between the infinity of the universe and the puny capacities of its finitude, turns with Camus into the anthropomorphic pride which naturally repudiates any Kierkegaardian leap into faith or Pascalian humility, and which not only repudiates God but 'dares the enormity of saying that the absurd is sin without God'. (*Ibid.*, p. 60) The Promethean dream of Camus breaks through this kind of statement which has neither the superhuman Nietzschean courage to declare God dead, nor the Sartrian clear-cut pride in declaring that man aspires to be God. Camus wants to have it both ways, and can never transcend his ethical ambiguities, his lurking longing for metaphysics, and his injured, slightly self-pitying pride that God, whether He is or not, has not taken the trouble to answer his question and thus bring him the certainty and moral comfort which he needs. So he will adopt the stoical Sisyphean attitude of endlessly pushing up his rock, conscious of his revolt, and his nobility in revolt, and finding in this attitude of swallowing, without making faces, the bitter pill that life has inflicted upon him, the hope that the onlookers around him will suppose him happy or credit him with happiness. Sisyphus leaves this to others, he merely accomplishes his task, forgetting that by accomplishing it in a way that could bring happiness upon him, he makes this action a source of value, the absence of which Camus deplores.

Camus, with disarming innocence, expects for him the kind of special treatment that has been meted out to no man except Christ; and he, of course, though a little Christ-like, not only refuses to have anything to do with religion, but harshly blames Kierkegaard, Jaspers, Chestov and other religious thinkers for having practised the famous *credo quia absurdum*—something that he, who thinks himself more rational than human reason can bear, will never practise. He totally ignores the Heideggerian lesson, as he ignored other philosophers' lessons, that the ultimate unintelligibility of the world or ultimate groundlessness of Being has to be accepted as a necessary and unavoidable limitation of man's finitude. He fails to apprehend the notion that finitude is basic to man, that it underlies all existential attributes of man, and that by definition, the finite cannot grasp the ultimate rationality of its own existential being, since this rationality is Being or Eternity which both informs it and enfolds it.

Camus tries to evolve a whole philosophy from his rather shaky notion of absurdity, and this philosophy, which he expounds with brilliant rhetorical skill and enthusiasm, carried great sway with the young of the 1950s generation, but little conviction with anyone who held his breath and took a cool look at his manifesto about the good and the noble embodied in the myth of Sisyphus. Myths are myths, complexes of affective truths valid for one ethnic group within a given context, but not for any other and at all times, except in a new form. Sisyphus, the poor, oppressed North African labourer exploited by the white colonialists, touches Camus' heart as it touches anyone to see, on the French side of the Mediterranean, so many samples of African Sisyphuses still ruthlessly exploited; but a moral attitude based on the love of the oppressed is not a philosophy that one could extract from Camus' *Myth of*

Sisyphus. The employers and exploiters are at liberty to suppose Sisyphus happy, for it suits them, but it is Sisyphus's judgment that should matter, and no outsider can make him happy or should judge him so. The work in which Camus displays with conviction and efficacity the morality and the love of man that fills his heart is *La Peste*, a novel in which human solidarity and devotion to helping the afflicted reach the depths of Christian purity and evoke the name of Simone Weil.

The conclusions that Camus draws from his awareness of the absurdity of the world are unconvincing and lacking in logic; they are merely wilful attitudes towards problems whose data are not quite coherent, and out of which, therefore, only personal solutions can arise. Camus refuses suicide—one wonders why— refuses the consolation of any religion that would mean an abdication of reason, and, clutching his notion of the absurd as a talisman for life, derives from it three principles that should enable him, if not to triumph, at least to lead a dignified and noble life. First of all, to live is to live the absurd, to accept it fully, and to bear this constantly in mind. This is an attitude of defiance or revolt, but towards what or whom remains difficult to ascertain. This revolt is 'the constant presence of man to himself. It is not projection forward, it is without hope. This revolt is the certainty of a crushing fate, without the resignation that should accompany it.' (*Ibid.*, p. 77) What this fate is, or who controls it, is difficult to know; anyway, it is not ancient fate, for that fate necessarily implied acceptance of its decisions.

So we are faced with a kind of meteoric man, coming from nowhere, aware of his nothingness, and able to remain faithful to himself by remaining constantly aware of the absurdity of his state. This lucidity confers upon him the next great truth and advantage of his accepted state—he is free. With the gods (God or other divinities) he could not be free. But shorn of these limitations, conscious of his hopeless condition, irremediably condemned to death, he is free. René on his rock defying the waves, rebellious Byron wracked by fever on his bed at Missolonghi, were not half as romantic as Sisyphus clutching the candle light of the absurd against all the winds of human rationality and marching towards waiting death. The third principle to be engraved over the mantelpiece of the absurdist, if he has one, is that one must multiply, with passion, one's lucid experiences. 'To feel as much as possible one's life, one's revolt and one's freedom, is to love, and to live as much as possible. Where lucidity reigns, a scale of values becomes useless.' (*Ibid.*, p. 87) 'The present and the succession of presents in front of a soul constantly conscious, that is the ideal of absurd man.' (*Ibid.*, p. 88)

To live as much as possible is the aim of absurd man, quantity not quality is what matters; in such a life, all attractions are of equal value, only their intensity matters, and of course, as Dostoyevsky showed in *The Brothers Karamazov*, there is probably nothing more intense than the glitter and the fall of the axe on an expectant head. Man is his own and only end, and 'in the absurd world, the value of a notion or of a life is measured by its lack of fecundity,' (*ibid.*, p. 96) that is to say its lack of hope of finality. All this, like everything else Camus has done, is admirably, fascinatingly expressed, in sentences that dazzle and obnubilate the logic of meaning, so that the reader emerges from them practically in the frame of mind of one who steps out of the big dipper—he has seen stars, he has whirled around in a daze, and once his feet are back on the earth, he does not know where he is. He must sit down and retread his journey step by step, shedding the glitter and the intoxicating reverberation of the words; and at the end of it all, he finds himself not quite echoing Verlaine's words, but certainly mumbling them slowly to himself: 'this is literature', with perhaps little else. But literature is creation, and creation, whether for the artist or the actor, is the great adventure, the means by which he clarifies his revolt, develops the spiritual forces that make man's dignity, and therefore truly lives the life of the absurd. So that this interpretation of the myth of Sisyphus is, in the end, an illustration of the philosophical views that Camus tried to express. This being said, my preference and admiration go, as I have already suggested, to the Camus of *La Peste* and other literary works.

8

Simone Weil and Pierre Teilhard de Chardin

Simone Weil

The notion of a religious thinker necessarily raises suspicions and unavoidable initial resistances. A religious thinker is taken to mean someone who thinks within the framework of a given religion, someone who therefore has, at the back of his mind, a theology and a set of dogmas which orientate his philosophical researches and pursuits and confine them to the boundaries of his theology and the beliefs of his Church. That is to my mind a definition as constricting and wilfully narrow, consequently pejorative, as the one that consists in describing a poet of Donne's or Eliot's range and stature as a religious poet. These two poets are religious, deeply religious, but they are primarily poets, and although their poetry is suffused with feelings and thoughts that testify to a constant awareness of man's relationship with God and to the constant presence of God's will in the workings of the universe, they deal with all sorts of deeply human problems and experiences that are not in any way turned into expositions of a given Church's point of view.

A zealous parson or a minister might write a poem to illustrate a theological aspect of his creed; a true poet who is also a religious poet will not write religious illustrations or expound religion in verse or poetry. He will write about his encounters with the truth, pursued by his imagination which, because of his religious nature, always sees man as part of the whole, as emanating from and returning to Being. It is the same for a philosopher who is religious, as Spinoza was religious, as Pascal or Kierkegaard were not only religious but deeply practising Christians, but who could not nevertheless be described as

religious philosophers without suggesting that their philosophy is
entirely devoted to expounding and commenting on theological
problems or aspects of their faith, while this is not exactly the
case.

Simone Weil (1909–43) belongs to this category; she is a
deeply religious thinker who devoted her short life to the search
for and preparation for the coming of God to her, and she
carried out this search not through systematic thinking but as a
being possessed by a flame that impelled all her energies towards
the awaited union with God; one could, strictly speaking, avoid
considering her as a philosopher. Yet to ignore her thought, her
presence among the forces that were and still are at work in the
twentieth century, would be to use the blinkers of pharisaism
and pedantry in order to avoid studying, and in my view admir-
ing, one of the purest and most shining geniuses of our age. The
word 'saint' has been often mentioned in connection with her,
and there is no doubt that few human beings have practised the
love of God, the absolute charity and compassion towards her
fellow beings which Simone Weil displayed during her short,
illness-ridden and tormented life. Whether she was a saint or
not, is not the problem; what seems to be certain is that, if one
confines genius to the suggestion of the extraordinary and the
unexplainable, the light that dazzles and compels admiration,
Simone Weil was unquestionably a genius of the rarest quality in
our time, at a moment when, as she said, 'the world needs saints
who have genius, just as much as a town that is overrun by the
plague needs doctors.' (*Attente de Dieu*, Colombe, 1950, p. 105)
We are not overrun by the plague, but we are overrun by other
diseases that no doctors can cure, and we certainly need genius
of the Simone Weil type, so as to show us the inanity of vain
agitation, the uselessness of the love of profit-making, the
dehumanisation of mechanisation, and the increasing cleavage
between man and man; we need people like Simone Weil to
show—by their example, their endurance, their transmutation
of suffering and affliction into a humble acceptance of whatever
happens and unquenchable love—what it takes to bring peace
and happiness to our world.

Her philosophy, rooted in Greek thought, which she profoundly knew and understood, embraces all aspects of human

life, from politics to the arts, for inspiration, whether religious
or poetic, drinks from the same source. The universalism of the
Greeks pervades her thought, and this universalism marks
Eastern and Western thought, and makes of God's progressive
revelation to the world a journey that goes from the *Iliad* to the
Gospels, and connects Heraclitus, Socrates and Plato with Christ.
Her philosophy is not exclusive but syncretic; it unites, it
embraces all men in the same gaze, and it looks upon God as
a Father Who, throughout time, has appeared to His creatures in
the guise in which they were and are fit to recognise and to
welcome Him. It is a very sane and rational view, much more
so than any notion of Divine discrimination, such as that of a
chosen people and special treatments, which are unworthy of the
Divine. The Divine necessarily adjusts itself to the human, for
it is the Divine which always goes to the human and not the
other way round—the finite never being able to apprehend its
needs or to achieve the readiness required to receive the infinite
and to commune with it. Simone Weil's relations with God are
of the order of those of the great mystics—her prayer leaves us
breathless : 'Father, you who are pure goodness, and I who am
mediocrity, tear away my soul from my body for your own use,
and let nothing else survive except this tearing apart, or nothingness.' (*La Connaissance Surnaturelle*, Gallimard, 1950, p. 205)

Like Kierkegaard, Simone Weil believed that a witness to
truth is a martyr, and she believed, with Malebranche, that
attention is a prayer which the mind addresses to truth. The
search for truth was her central preoccupation, and this search
required a greater and greater shedding of desires, needs,
demands of the senses, and in the end of the body itself. The
body was an impediment to the journey of the soul, and deeply
Platonic as she was, she believed with Plato that 'Those who
pursue, as it should be done, the search for wisdom, do not do
anything else except practise how to die and how to be dead.'
(*Phaedo*) The final union with God implied the spiritual or
material disappearance of the body, and during the last years of
her life, Simone Weil increasingly practised this detachment
from the body which prefigures the final union with God. She
did so believing in the infinite compassion of God for suffering
and for all the afflictions of man. Yet, she said time and time

again that misfortune must not be chosen, and that too much of it crushes man like a worm and submerges the soul in terror. Christ Himself, overwhelmed by suffering, felt forsaken and was for a moment forlorn. Attention and obedience to God are what matters, and God comes and inhabits the one who loves Him and can love himself only through Him. Simone Weil's life could be summed up by this thought from Master Eckhart: 'If man through his obedience renounces himself, then God will necessarily enter him, for in truth for the one who desires nothing for himself, God must desire in the same way as for Himself.' Man must not imagine that he can put holiness into his work, he must put holiness into himself, for it is not the works that sanctify him, it is he who must sanctify the works.

We may be told that this is not quite philosophy but mysticism, tragic living in the expectation of grace and Divine visitation, something that cannot be explained, assessed or defined. Yet to ignore this kind of man-to-man relationship, and man's relationship to the Divine, would be to seek refuge in superficial rationalism and to behave like ostriches before great human needs, which can be met only by enriching human experiences whose type of truth has as much importance for the life of man as those that can be assessed and organised by the sophistications of reason.

Teilhard de Chardin

With Teilhard de Chardin (1881–1955) we are, as in the case of Simone Weil, on the periphery of philosophy, in the domain of lived philosophy, or of philosophy as a dramatisation of the human consciousness, and Teilhard de Chardin, scientist, priest and mystic, has tried to bridge the widening gap between science and religion and to reconcile both. His attempt has, in some cases, brought upon him the anger of the devotees of specialisation, either in science or in philosophy, and he has been taken to task by both. He has in fact endured the fate of all those who have been unable to resist the lure of the great questions prompted by life, and he has dared to face up to them. Arnold Toynbee, whose brilliant synthesis of the rise and fall of civilisations is now more and more accepted as a work of genius, had first to withstand the sneers and barbed criticism of all those who could not dissociate the notion of history from that of facts. Yet, what is a fact? We have now ceased asking this meaning-less question, at least we have ceased to weigh or measure facts purely with mathematical instruments; we know that there are all sorts of facts, and that we have to deal with them according to the field or the area to which they belong. The problem of the meaning of meaning, and other cognate problems of logic and linguistics, are very real and important ones which men have a duty to probe, but these problems can concern only a few who are endowed with the specialised knowledge to pursue them, while questions such as : why is there life? and : what is life? haunt most men's minds, and whether they are verifiable, falsifi-able, or could or could not logically be asked, is irrelevant.

Logic does not control the beating of the heart and of the anxious mind, and if these questions are necessarily asked, it is normal that attempts to answer them should be made. True enough, Nietzsche has declared God dead, and more adventurous minds have even declared man himself dead, leaving behind only a vague self-caused entity called language. But the world is preoccupied by more wide-ranging and basic problems, and the uncertainty of its present, the anguish of its future, cannot be dispelled by messages from the moon or from Venus, or from laurelled scientists from their laboratories. None of these messages brings any warmth to the heart or puts an end to its questioning. The Cross did not bring an answer, for if it had done so, the world would have been different; yet, at least it gave man the hope that it was worth searching and trudging on, for, in spite of its fearful limitations and shortcomings, mankind, part of a rational creation, is neither a useless passion nor an absurd Sisyphean performance up and down a barren hill. The Cross may be fading away on the horizon, yet man continues to long for a light and a guiding hope and a new Jerusalem which, though beyond logic, is deeply real.

The point is : What does Teilhard de Chardin's thought mean to the modern world? What does it contribute to modern man's experience? What questions does it answer that the dream of science and technology cannot answer? What effect does his thought have on the life of man? These are very important questions, and whether one calls his attitude to life and to man's relations to Being a philosophy or an ideology, the problem of its relationship to the society of its time, and to that of times to come, is a measure of its importance and worth. Marxism is only an ideology, irreducible to the demands of totally scientific method, yet no other ideology, except that which concerns the various types of relationship of being to Being, is more important. Such reflections make it evident that Teilhard de Chardin's thought could not be ignored, and that one must therefore try to assess its true intrinsic value, irrespective of the impossibility of categorising it.

Teilhard de Chardin was a paleontologist trained in the scientific disciplines of his age who, through his scientific researches and observations, was led to the conclusion that the world is one, and that the evolution of life on earth rests upon invariables and upon a very specific type of finality that leads to the absolute spiritualisation of matter. These views are not very original, and one can easily connect them with aspects of Plato, of Hegel, with Bergson's philosophy which synthesised aspects of Hegelianism and evolutionism, and also with the metaphysics of Christianity. Teilhard's unfolding of the process of evolution, particularly the transition from biosphere to noosphere, to say nothing of his metaphysical speculations on the nature of being, are arguable, and they have attracted both devoted admiration and fierce opposition from some scientists, who seem to have thought they sensed in his deeply human attempt to reconcile science and religion a kind of betrayal. This is very sad, for as one of the founding heroes of the scientific world—Copernicus—said, God wants man, as far as it is possible for him to do so, to know the truth of things. Scientific truth can only be part of the rationality of creation, and the only points to bear in mind are that human truth is finite, relativistic, progressive, and has many facets, even although they are related to one central one.

Teilhard has become a social phenomenon that no pseudo-scientific sleight of hand and pejorative epithets can dispose of. His main works, *The Phenomenon of Man* (1955) and *The Divine Milieu* (1957), have become bestsellers, in an age when such results are reserved not for poetry and great novels, but for superficial novels and pornographic literature. The cult and exegesis of his writings and thought has brought into existence numerous Teilhard de Chardin societies and conferences all over the world, and these conferences and societies are patronised by the greatest scientists of our time, so that it is difficult to dismiss him as appealing only to the *literati*, the religion-obsessed or those thirsting for mysticism and occultism. The solid scientific basis of some of his researches precludes such pejorative comments. No modern religious figure since Cardinal Newman has had the influence that Teilhard de Chardin has had on the religious thought and life of his time, and this widespread enthusiasm for his thought, deplored by some, welcomed by others, is due to the fact that in an age of scepticism, anxiety and fear of the unknown, Teilhard has brought to man the comforting thought that God is neither above nor below, nor confined to churches and monasteries, but present everywhere in the life of man and the life of the universe, and that He expects us to love Him, not in the seclusion of our hearts, indifferent to the misery and suffering of others, but through our endeavours to apply His principle of love and brotherhood to the everyday life of His creation and through trying to spiritualise and to transform it here and now, instead of waiting for a distant supra-earthly heaven. It is this philosophy of religion in action which obviously attracts Marxists to Teilhardism, and this attraction which results in the tempering of Marxist materialism with the Christian respect for the sacredness of the individual, can only be beneficent to mankind. For, although some of Marx's ideas have been by now digested, discarded or absorbed by twentieth-century society, others, particularly those that coincide with the basic Christian creed that all men should have an equal share in the fruits of the earth, or should not be deprived of the fruits of their labour, are still very much alive, because they remain practically unfulfilled the world over.

Modern Marxism looks upon religion as a superstructure of history, and not as an alienation of man's best qualities and aspirations, as Marx, following Feuerbach, had defined it. If religion is looked upon not as alienation but as one of the superstructures of history, then Marxists will not find it difficult to co-operate with it in activities that aim at transforming human history. Teilhard does not separate matter from spirit and the human from the Divine; his aim is to sanctify human activities or to spiritualise matter, so that a Marxist can find agreement with him if he gives to the word 'sanctification' a purely humanistic meaning that confers upon human labour its deserved value and power which will enable it to transform the world. The Marxist naturally cannot share Teilhard's view that man's urge to transform the world is basic to man as a being who carries within himself the historical sense of his individual worth as God's creature; but he shares with him the sense of the historical value of the process of change, the social basis of human relations, a common evolutionism, a common social altruism and a desire to change the world through action. For Teilhard, religion is an activity of life; for Marxists life is action to transform history into the final abolition of history. For Teilhard, Christ the *logos* is at the centre of the evolution of the world, and anyone who serves Christ serves the good of man. Teilhard realised that the Church had to get out of its Victorian walls and conventions, and preach God's presence on earth, and not in some all-too-distant new Jerusalem. He felt that the earthly hopes of men, which do not exclude hopes of heaven, had to be met on earth, and that scientific progress and its beneficent effects were part of God's love for men and should not be dissociated from man's love for God.

Whatever one may think of Teilhard's specifically scientific achievements, or of the logic of his philosophy, the greatness of his mind, the breadth of his vision, cannot be denied. In a world deprived of God by science and pseudo-rational scepticism, he understood that God had to come down to earth, to live among men and to answer their crying needs. For him, man is the apex, or the guiding light of creation, and his duty is to spiritualise his activities more and more, so that creation may come nearer and nearer to the noosphere, the realm of pure being.

Spiritualisation does not mean turning away from life or from matter, but on the contrary activity in life and the spiritualisation of matter which is the very stuff of God's creation and an integral part of His purpose, carried out by the continuous presence of Christ among men. Every man is in some way Christ, and to ill-treat him, to diminish him, is to ill-treat and to diminish Christ, and through Him, God Himself. The dynamics of these beliefs are of the utmost importance for the life of mankind. Whether the noosphere can or cannot be charted or quantified through scientific processes, the evolutionary theories of Teilhard de Chardin are scientifically based, and the effects of his beliefs and the finality he assigns to evolution are, if not scientifically measurable, undeniably inspiring and ethically beneficent in their application to life. Teilhard's synthetic view of the universe carries weaknesses and untenable notions, but this does not detract from the strength of his moral purpose and from the validity of large stretches of his phenomenological observations and conclusions. He was himself aware of his limitations, but he knew that truth in its entirety does not belong to any man, and that everyone can only contribute his share, and he was more aware than most of the vital ontological problems that confront modern man.

For Teilhard there is no opposition between religion and science. The foreword of *The Phenomenon of Man* states that it is 'a scientific memoir'; and, like Bergson, he insists that he will stick to scientific methods. Like Bergson, he says that science deals with the phenomenal reality of things, and that his final aim is to pass from phenomenal reality or the biosphere to the noosphere or the ultimate reality of creation. The noosphere represents the unification and coherence of mind, the final interiorisation or spiritualisation of matter, through an energising, ascending noogenesis opposing entropy, and giving meaning and direction to evolution. The spiritualisation of matter is Bergsonian, and the finality that animates evolution is a self-contained dynamism and not an external, intervening force. The noosphere enfolds the union of man and spirit or mind, which is a union of multiplicities and not an absolute Hegelian whole. It is the biosphere or matter which has reached a high degree of spiritualisation and consciousness of the finality of evolution. This finality does not exclude efficient causes, biological mutations and adjustments. It is merely confined to the basic attributes of matter or orthogenesis.

Orthogenesis is, according to Teilhard, 'the law of guided complexification which governs the process of change of the micromolecules and megamolecules from which the first cells

were evolved'. (*Le Phénomène Humain*, Le Seuil, 1955, p. 114)
He confines the meaning of this term purely to biology, and
rejects for it any connection with metaphysical finality. He distinguishes a fundamental antinomy between entropy—the law
of the degradation of energy—and biological orthogenesis or
energy which animates evolutive creation, which is pulled apart
between these two tendencies and has to reconcile them, so that,
in the end, in spite of the degradation of energy, the law of
orthogenesis maintains a growing capacity for complexification
and for increasing consciousness. Life, for Teilhard, is animated
by two types of energy—radial or spiritual energy which is the
ascending, complexifying energy, and tangential material energy
which tends to maintain together all the elements of the same
order of complexity that belong to the same field. This latter
energy resists change and tends towards stabilisation, and the
resistance to change is in proportion to the radial energy, so that
radial energy can only progress through wearing down tangential
energy, as required by the law of entropy. The dialectical interplay of these two types of energy carries, nevertheless, the pre-
eminence of one of the two, which is radial energy. This
pre-eminence is basic to Being, for Being is not dualism but oneness, and not a duality of Being and non-Being. So the radial
energy which is the cause of life is basic to or among the
properties of the primal molecules that formed the first cell of
life, while the tangential energy has, with regard to the radial
energy, the kind of relationship that non-being has to being; it
derives from it as its dialectical element necessary to the process
for finally reaching Being.

Teilhard looked upon science and religion as being 'the twin
sisters of humanity'. (*Ibid.*, p. 276) He looked upon himself as
a scientist, and as such he was aware, like Pascal, that there are,
besides mathematical certainties, other certainties. As a scientist,
he was well aware of the strength of the second principle of
thermodynamics. The world, for him, was not static but in
continuous evolution towards what he called the omega point
—a questionable notion which does not nevertheless invalidate
his concept of evolution, which is a concept of unified action
involving heaven and earth, matter and spirit, body and soul, to
the extent that Teilhard said that if ever he stopped one day

believing in God, he would still go on believing in the world, for
it was God-created. He had a Franciscan, some wrongly said a
pantheistic, love for the earth and for all things created. The
earth about which he spoke in lyrical terms had been, for him,
shaped by God's hands, something best suggested by Blake's
pictorial genius. Thence Teilhard's philosophy of action and
active participation in life.

For him, to confine oneself to spiritual life, to fail to act and
to play one's part in the life of mankind, was a refusal to participate in God's active creation. Purity is not reduced to an absence
of failures and to non-action; it is, on the contrary, measured by
the urge that impels man to help other men, and turns him
towards the Divine centre of spirituality. This is not obtained
through quietism or resignation to evil, but through action and
resistance to evil to the very limits of our human possibilities.
We do not, according to Teilhard, reach God in passivity and
withdrawal from life, we meet Him at the intersecting point
between our active energy and the resistance that is opposed to
our efforts to contribute as best we can to the reduction of multiplicity into oneness and Divine simplicity. Far from detracting
from man's concentration on his earthly task, Teilhard believed,
like St Bernard, that this was a way of paying homage to God
by consciously co-operating in His creation. For Teilhard, Christ
and the incarnation is what truly matters. 'Through the incarnation which has saved men, the very becoming of the universe
has been transformed and sanctified.' (*Ecrits du Temps de la
Guerre*, Grasset, 1965, p. 49)

The incarnation spiritualises matter, transforms and makes of
action and life in time the means of reaching the eternal.
Through the incarnation, the omnipresent activity of God is
carried out through the omnipresence of Christ Who gathers in
His mystical body all the spiritual values of the actions and
suffering of anyone who acts in communion with Him. If, for
those who are in rebellion against theological terminology, we
replace Christ by the notion of being as the becoming of Being,
we can, in purely philosophical terms, understand the notion of
goodness as a more or less perfect participation in the awareness
of Being. Man, for Teilhard, sums up and assumes the universe;
he is, through his capacity to know and to be conscious of him-

self, the crowning element of the evolutionary process of creation, and through his love and his purpose, he contributes by his own spiritualisation to the spiritualisation of the universe. Man's soul, inseparable from his earthly life, participates in the making of and the giving of a meaning to creation, through his adhesion to Christ. Through creation, matter and the human are transfigured, not into a perfect Hegelian absolute in which the multiple is practically absorbed into the one, but into a form of oneness which has not completely abolished individual identity. The individual has a responsibility towards society which is part of the oneness of creation, pervaded by the mystical body of Christ, and he participates, through love, in the being of Being which is Christ. The incarnation, for Teilhard, not only implies the redemption of sin, but also the Divine completion of creation, and of man in the love of God. Christ is the subsistence, apex or omega of the universe, and His grace and participation in life apply to the body as well as to the soul, without any possible dualism between the one and the other.

Every living being endeavours to make his soul or his eternal essence through his human activities, for God accomplishes Himself in action, and He has accepted death in order to make it clear that man has to go through night to return to light. For Teilhard, Christ's body is the world in which we are physically and biologically united, and the world's task is the physical incorporation of the faithful into Christ. This stress upon the importance of the body relates Teilhard to phenomenologists like Merleau-Ponty and existentialists of the type represented by Gabriel Marcel. The world has been created in Christ, said St Paul, and Teilhard tried to show phenomenologically how creation is a process of unification and spiritualisation which is the accomplishment of the Divine plan to sanctify nature. 'Through every one of our works we endeavour to construct the Pleroma, that is to say to add something to the completion of Christ. Each of our works, through the more or less distant repercussions that it has upon the spiritual world, contributes to perfecting Christ in His mystical totality.' (*Le Milieu Divin*, Le Seuil, 1957, p. 5)

The Western world, more and more dominated by the bourgeoisie, had ended up looking upon Christianity as a set of values intended to ensure the salvation of that bourgeoisie and the protection of their own egotistical interests and material possessions. Church practice, or even the mere appearances of the practice of religion, were quite enough. Teilhard clearly understood that this was the end of religion, for religion can only be participation in and attention to the earthly needs as well as the spiritual needs of man, as God's creature. Teilhard's concept of evolution as a continuous process of complexification and spiritualisation implies a concept of evil that has caused a good deal of disquiet in Church orthodoxy. Yet it is by far the most rational notion of evil that one could think of, for the traditional notion of original sin has always been an incomprehensible and intractable notion. Teilhard rightly recognises that the passage from the multiple to the one cannot take place without losses, diminutions, rejections and suffering, which are generally described under the name of evil; yet, evil is nothing more than the old Hegelian notion of negation and opposition to Being. The multiple necessarily tends towards dispersion and limitations which have to be transcended by a unifying cause. 'The essence of Christianity is nothing more nor less than the belief in the unification of the world in God, through the incarnation.' (*L'Energie Humaine*, Le Seuil, 1962, p. 113)

Evil is coextensive with time as a limitation or diminution of Being; it is the necessary fallout of being, it flows as negation from the positiveness of being which, through consciousness, absorbs and transforms it into positive energy. 'Human suffering, the totality of suffering floating at any moment over the face of the earth, what an immense ocean it constitutes! What is this mass made of? Black deeds, failures, rejects? Not at all; it is made of possible energies. In suffering lies hidden, and endowed with an extreme intensity, the ascending force of the world. The whole problem is to free this force by giving it the consciousness of what it means and what it can do.' (*Hymne de l'Univers*, Le Seuil, 1961, p. 100) The suffering and calamities of the world are the necessary lining of being, which has primacy over them, and which, therefore, transforms the fragmentations and particularisations of existence into oneness. The existent can hope to reach oneness only through death, or at the very extreme point of tension between being and non-being, when the individuated consciousness bends all its energy to reach being and merge with it. 'To understand the world, knowledge is not enough; one must see, touch, live in the presence of, and drink existence from the very heart of Reality.' (*Ibid.*, p. 67) This is a very Bergsonian thought which, in order to give an idea of what was previously meant by the existent's attempts to reach oneness, could be completed by this sentence : 'I know that the Divine will only be revealed to me at the extreme limit of my effort. Like Jacob, I shall only truly touch God in His reality when I have been defeated by Him.' (*Ibid.*, p. 27)

Teilhard is, as noted earlier, in many respects Hegelian. History moves according to the laws of its component elements, and man, more and more conscious of its direction, takes command of this direction, so that in Hegelian or Marxist fashion, history totalises itself to disappear as history. Christ, or the incarnation, has come to transform the world and to bring all things to oneness. Christ—first born, ever reborn—and the earth will be united, for the earth will become both the body of the one who is and of the one who comes.

This active participation of Christ, God's incarnation, in creation has often caused Teilhard de Chardin to be accused of pantheism. Yet it is not so. In Teilhard's philosophy, God is distinct from creation and is not one with it. God is neither the earth, nor an alternative to it. The earth is God-made, and man, part of it, must, in accord with God, free from egoism and self-interest, make it fit for Christ's presence. Teilhard loves the earth which is the body of Christ, and as such it must, according to him, be pervaded with justice, equality and love among men, so that life may have a meaning and a sense of direction. He does not try to prove what cannot be proved, but he tries to convince men that, in the light of faith, the world would look different, and that the inner forces of man's consciousness can transform matter. 'God only emerges as the universal milieu, because it is the ultimate point towards which all reality converges. God is infinitely near, and spread everywhere, just because He is the centre that occupies the whole sphere.' (*Le Milieu Divin*, p. 136) Every life is sustained by Christ, and man is called upon to co-create and to participate in the sanctification and spiritualisation of the world. Teilhard teaches us care for all

men—the poor, the weak, the disinherited in the West as well
as in the third world, all part of Christ, and his life and writings
are an inspiration to all those who think like him. 'In truth, how
numerous are those among us, who nurse in the bottom of their
hearts the mad hope of a transformation of our earth! . . . Let
us look around us on earth. What happens under our eyes,
among masses of people? Whence this social unrest, this anxiety,
these swelling waves, these eddies which converge, these terrifying new upsurges? Humankind is going through a crisis in its
growth. It is obscurely aware of what it lacks and of what it
can do. In front of it, as we have said in the first pages of this
book, the universe becomes luminous, like the horizon where the
sun is about to rise. Mankind foresees and therefore waits. . . .
To desire the Parousia, we have only to Christianise and let beat
in us the very heart of the earth.' (*Ibid.*, pp. 199–201)

9

Epistemology: Gaston Bachelard

The world of Gaston Bachelard (1884–1962) belongs more to the epistemology of science and the arts than to epistemology as a well-established branch of philosophy. His importance in the domain of literature could not be overstressed. Irrespective of the claims of the new critics and the *nouveau roman*, French criticism, from Marcel Raymond to Albert Béguin, Georges Poulet, Starobinski or J.-P. Richard is, consciously or subconsciously, inspired by or in accord with the theories of Bachelard. These theories are positively and negatively connected with Bergsonian and Jamesian philosophy, and they have deep roots in Western thought. They go back to German, French and English romanticism, to Novalis, Coleridge and Mme de Staël, and they rest upon Coleridge's famous theory of empathy and upon Rousseau's abolition of the Cartesian *cogito* and its absorption into the unifying ripples of the sensation that merges the *I* of the subject into the thing apprehended or perceived, continuing Baudelaire's approach to the work of art, and above all the Bergsonian notion of duration applied to criticism. They are the last attempt to assert the importance of diachronicity and individual consciousness, before structuralist neo-positivism and pseudo-objectivism based on linguistics take over.

Like Bergson, Bachelard trusts both in reason and in imagination. Reason is supreme in scientific knowledge, while imagination is so in the domain of the inner reality of things and in the arts, and the two are not opposed but complementary, one being the lining of the other, in order to achieve a complete knowledge of reality. Bachelard's rationalism is fundamentally anti-Cartesian, that is to say it is not continuous and centred around an unchanging or rather an ever-reborn *cogito*, apprehending and unifying the various aspects of extended reality, but discontinuous and above all dialectical. Neither truth nor reason are looked upon as immutable Platonic entities; truth is relativistic and dialectical, and reason is praxis. Science and knowledge move diachronically and dialectically through negations and new syntheses, as parts of a world that is never closed, but that is on the contrary always open to wonderment, to new interpretations and new unveilings of truth in fields in which they remain valid for a given time. It is therefore a dynamic world, a world in a state of active evolution, in which the artist is a continuously changing subject projecting himself towards the future, and thus continuously modifying the object of his search which is a given aspect of the truth.

Knowledge is not a matter of a fixed object apprehended by an unchanging subject or *cogito*, but a question of fluid, ever-evolving relationships between the phenomenal world and an apprehending subject. We are back to Bergsonian relativism and flux which makes of rational truth a synthesis of negations and an absorption of concepts into new relationships valid for a given time and place. 'The problem of error seemed to us to have pre-eminence over the problem of truth, or one could say that we have found no possible solution to the problem of truth except by discarding smaller and smaller errors.' (G. Bachelard, *Essai sur la Connaissance Approchée*, Vrin, 1928, p. 244) Truth is not static but the result of the continuous activity of changing human reason, and this notion of action and creativity extends to the critical imagination which conforms to the Schopenhauerian notion of criticism and appreciation of the arts as creativity. Thought works out its own categories, and truth is a product of man's mind, therefore it is always related to the thinking subject as a social being who constructs, rectifies or rejects it in the course of a continuous action. Science also is never static; it implies continuous research and continuous uncertainty and wonderment, as part of a dialectical praxis in search of the truth which is never given, but always obtained through the elimination of ignorance and errors.

There is no fixed Platonic truth waiting to be discovered. Bachelard, more post-Hegelian than he acknowledges, looks upon truth as being progressively uncovered through moments of active subjectivity which becomes aware of its true being or connection with transcendental intersubjectivity. This search for truth is an essentially humanistic and changing activity of negation and absorption; it is a dialectical process which constantly asserts itself against, and also absorbs into itself, parts of what it has been. It is a continuous voyage of discovery without a fixed *cogito* to organise and carry out the journey, and without a fixed goal towards which to move; for, just as in art, the goal is truly known only once it has been reached. This search is therefore truly objective in the sense that it is not conceptually guided; it is an anxiety to know, an openness towards an aim which, once reached, is the moment of truth or knowledge which contains object and subject, and must be abandoned for new pursuits, for otherwise this object objectifies itself, precludes new anxieties and hopes of new discoveries, and becomes a fixed pattern of beliefs or thought, or a persona which the artist or the thinker accepts, instead of continuing to search for the truth. Truth is the 'creux toujours futur, aux sources du poème, entre le vide et l'événement pur' of Valéry; it is like Odysseus' Ithaca, always beyond the crest of the next wave, and whether in science or in the arts, Bachelard believes in the constant activity of reason and of the imagination, moving with the shifting virtualities of scientific or artistic truth.

He could probably say, paraphrasing King Lear, that the readiness is all; but readiness is merely a concept, and in order that there may be readiness there must be some cause or subsistence behind it, and that is where the problem lies, for however objective or non-subjective this Bachelardian search for truth may be, it implies a something that sustains it, and as this something cannot be the rejected Cartesian *cogito*, it must nevertheless be an essence or form, or a becoming towards being and knowing through actualisation, which becomes the moment of perfect self-knowledge, lost as soon as achieved, yet not forgotten and remaining therefore a constant source of inspiration for new actualisations and further knowledge. 'These moments', says Bachelard, 'are moments of the dawning of knowledge, and intellectual courage consists in making of them the inexhaustible sources of our intentions.' (*L'Intuition de l'Instant*, Stock, 1935, p. 9) Needless to say, these moments of perfect self-knowledge, that is to say moments of awareness of true being, rejoin the Bergsonian duration, the mystic's awareness of God's will, and also Nietzsche's notion of the eternal return as pure positive being, freed from all its negations.

Bachelard's main prerequisite for the discovery of truth is a state of innocence and receptivity which implies a kind of continuously newly-born consciousness, and whether it works in the light of reason or in the night of dreams or 'rêverie' from which intuition or imagination shapes its formulations in art, consciousness is what matters. This consciousness is neither an epiphenomenon of matter nor a purely spiritual Cartesian *cogito* apprehending and shaping matter as if it were completely separated from it. It is neither Bergsonian consciousness struggling to mould matter, nor the Sartrian nothingness or *for-itself* intent upon turning itself into an *in-itself* and desperately entangled in the viscosity and materiality of things, therefore condemned to the failure that makes of existence 'une passion inutile'. Bachelard's consciousness does not fear materiality, petrification, transformation into the *in-se* of repellent animality. On the contrary, he feels that it is inextricably woven into matter which, whatever its appearance, its phenomenal manifestations perceived by the senses, is the basis for imaginative creation and self-knowledge. With him, phenomenology is the foundation of ontology, and in that respect he connects with Bergson, Husserl and Merleau-Ponty.

Bachelard's protean genius cannot be fitted into any clear-cut category. He is neither a philosopher nor a scientist nor a poet, yet no one in our time has explored more thoroughly and more deeply the workings of the imagination, the source of artistic creation and the metamorphoses of matter apprehended phenomenologically. 'Only phenomenology—that is to say the examination of the starting point of the image in an individual consciousness—can help us to restore the subjectivity of the image and to measure the force and the meaning of the transsubjectivity of the image.' (*La Poétique de l'Espace*, Presses Universitaires de France, 1957, p. 5) This is an entirely new approach to art, in twentieth-century France. For Sainte-Beuve, Faguet, Lemaître or Lanson, the text is a pretext for biographical introspections, impressionistic disquisitions or abstract notions of pendulum-like artistic movements, and filiations and paternities. I exclude, of course, Baudelaire who, like Coleridge, knew that criticism could not be reduced to such superficial attitudes. In England, the Coleridgean tradition has remained constantly alive right up to modern times, and names like those of Caroline Spurgeon, Wilson Knight, Livingston Lowes, Leavis and Eliot testify to the concern for the search for the thematic and metaphoric structures that underlie the framework of the poetic image and the poetic imagination.

Bachelard is aware that between the concept—the instrument of scientific knowledge, and the image—the instrument of poetic knowledge, there is no possibility of synthesis, and that therefore the problem for the critic is to place himself in the depths or at the birth of the sensation that he will try to apprehend in its freshness and purity, and to follow through its complexifications, developments and formalisations, without ever being anything else but an observing and recording subjectivity. To try to objectify the growth and organicity of creative subjectivity so as to study it as an object is to destroy it and, in the end, to study the appearance of a dead thing. Life cannot be objectified, it can only be observed by adhering to its unforeseeable movements and developments, until it meets death which arrests it and turns it into a thing or an object, amenable to scientific knowledge and observation. Therefore the critical consciousness must endeavour to merge into the images and sensations suggested by the words, become what they are, and be expressed by them as part of a unified and harmonised, Rousseauesque world in which the creative consciousness itself has become part of this world which lives and speaks through it.

In these states of inspiration, awakened dreaming or whatever one likes to call them, the conscious and the subconscious merge and pervade the objects, the images and the sensations in which they fix themselves and through which they reveal their being. There is no longer a subject and an object, there is only a living subjectivity expressing its being through the world of the imagination. The awareness of being rests, not upon the intellect, but upon fluctuating sensations fed by the imagination, constantly moving on the verge of being and non-being, and bringing out of the subconscious and non-being an awareness of being that has not been intellectually processed and that still trails behind it the shadows and deep roots of its materiality. Matter for Bachelard is the material upon which creative imagination works, and it is the element that renders apprehensible the notions of space and time. Without it there would be only pure spirit, eternal radiance in the unstained oneness of Eternity.

The reality of being can be apprehended only, as Bergson pointed out, through intuition or imagination, and creativeness, which expresses being, can be apprehended only by reliving the journey of the creative imagination, its imaginary world and its enthusiasms, through a state of perfect receptivity and purity. Criticism is therefore participation in the creative act; it is reliving this act as a subject knowing what it is to be both a creating and an observing subject. Criticism implies, in Bachelard's view, the identification of the *I* of the critic with that of the creator, and at the same time the capacity to relive the process of the creative act, from the inside, while noting down, without any conscious intrusion or interference, the flow of the sensations caused by the work's images on the critic's own consciousness. This requires dedication, humility and the imagination and empathy that enable the critic to place his own self in as perfect as possible a harmony with the creator's subjectivity, whose imaginative fluctuations he follows, so as to discover what the work of art truly is, and what it reveals at a given moment in time, and also as part of historical time.

IO

Structuralism:

Claude Lévi-Strauss, Michel Foucault, Louis Althusser

After Simone Weil who could not bear the existence of human suffering and misery without sharing them to the point of accepting a saintly death, after Teilhard de Chardin's dream of Christ-centred, love-illumined earth, after the silence of the last philosopher, Sartre, whose humanism seems now to be a voice in the wilderness, philosophy, in France, seems to have been replaced by various aspects of epistemology, based above all on linguistics, made to provide analogies for anthropological, mythological and social patterns, including literature and religion. Three divinities look from afar upon these mental cogitations—Nietzsche, Marx and Freud, and for the sake of Lévi-Strauss, one could add J.-J. Rousseau.

Nietzsche gave the lead by proclaiming the death of God, which was necessarily followed by the death of man, since all man's values finally rested on Him, and man cannot therefore live, or at least be what he was, without God. Marx transferred these alienated values onto man and onto history, but since the silence of Sartre and in spite of the soundly argued protests of Raymond Aron, Marx can now be accepted only as a structuralist or not at all—at least so it is for many French intellectuals. Freud himself does not remain unscathed, and his great cleavage of the human ethos into the *ego* and the *id*, the conscious and the subconscious, is reduced to binary manifestations of thought and abstract linguistic structure and compartmentations alien to the organicity of life at the natural as well as at the social level.

Every epoch needs a guru, an avatar, a leading figure. Sartre admirably fulfilled that role in the 1950s. Claude Lévi-Strauss (b. 1908) is that of the 1960s. He is the propounder of structural anthropology, and structuralism is the key-word to all disciplines. Jakobson's linguistics was already quietly structuralist, but there had not been much excitement about this aspect of linguistics until structuralism became the fashion. Now everything, from Marxism to literature, has to be structuralist, and by the wise men of the Left Bank of the Seine Racine and Flaubert are supposed, like Monsieur Jourdain who spoke prose without knowing it, to have been structuralists without being aware of it.

Linguistics, and anthropology in as far as it is not an ideology, do not come into the category of fleeting literary fashion. Linguistics is a serious discipline which is outside the theme of this work, while on the other hand anthropology, as serious a discipline as the other, is, in its philosophical aspect, a relevant part of its theme. Lévi-Strauss is an earnest, highly esteemed anthropologist, and the immoderate, and probably to him unwelcome, use of his basic discoveries in anthropology for literary arguments and theories does not detract from the importance of his work which has influenced researches in sociology, psychiatry and linguistics. Structuralism is a brand-new word, but if one looks, as we shall do, behind the appearances of the word, we shall see that it covers very old forms of human thought which range from Plato to Spinoza, Kant and contemporary existentialism. It would be unnatural if the matter were otherwise, and in fact structuralism itself postulates the perenniality of human thought and of the human mind, which precludes absolute novelty. Working backwards through history—a process of which anti-evolutionist structuralists disapprove—one can see at once that structuralism has, notwithstanding marked differences, some common roots with Marxism. Whilst Marxist structures reflect social and economic forces, for the structuralist these forces emanate from the subconscious, and they are, like myths, linguistic entities, keys to various aspects of thought and behaviour.

History is the present, that is to say the present-present, and the past in the present, gathered into one single instant of consciousness, moving back and forth diachronically in time, or transporting itself from time present into time past. But history is time, and for the structuralist there is no single time. There are various times, all synchronic, as there are various spaces, or various fields of relationships or of structures which are strictly topological. Both the historian and the anthropologist try to think the possible. The historian knows when history began, and the way it has unfolded, he therefore works backwards towards its progressive discovery. The anthropologist always places himself in the present and tries, by a combination of facts and hypotheses, to work out the possible. The historian lives the past; his quest is Proustian; it is that of *le temps retrouvé*. Structuralism is the search for the fundamental, symbolic patterns or structures of life in all its manifestations. Once one knows the true structures of life, one can improve it.

As an anthropologist, Lévi-Strauss starts from the principle that nothing in life is gratuitous or absurd; everything, for him, is part of a total coherence and has meaning. 'The meaning of men's dwellings goes beyond that which pertains to being the centre of social and religious life, which I have tried to describe. The structure of the village does something more than make possible the refined working of the institution. It both sums up and insures the relationships between man and the universe, society and the supernatural world, and between the living and the dead.' (*Tristes Tropiques*, Plon, 1955, p. 197) Starting from these premises, Lévi-Strauss generally endeavours to establish a model to which he seeks to relate the data he discovers. This approach is not, in certain aspects, unscientific, since Karl Popper accepts it as being the preliminary hypothesis which has to be verified or falsified by facts; yet of course, it is a method of approach to knowledge that ignores the concrete and the particular, and runs counter to empiricism which prefers to start with factual knowledge.

Lévi-Strauss's model must fulfil at least three conditions:

1) It must possess the main characteristic of a system, which is that if one aspect of this system is modified, the whole of it is also modified.

2) Its properties must make it possible to know how the model will react if one of its elements is modified.

3) The model must account for all the observed facts.

Every structure is a model; empirical reality consists in a more or less exact conformity with given models, and societies themselves are dominated by models as transcendental and immanent patterns which they reproduce. We are not back to Plato's cave, but the shades of Plato are certainly not far off. Nature, for Lévi-Strauss, aspires towards culture, and in linguistic terms this means that the object tends towards the sign and towards language. This is one of the aspects of a binary world, or of the to-and-fro of life as seen by Lévi-Strauss. Another aspect is that, starting from the sign, from the linguistic representation of the object, one should be able to discover the hidden properties of this object, the structure of the model to which it belongs, and, going even further, since all of this is related to the human mind, the mode of functioning of the human mind. Human brains are natural objects, part of nature, therefore they must, like all aspects of nature, share universal characteristics, while cultures, being the product of the human brain, must necessarily share traits and structures. These structures seem to be well established philosophical notions, in some ways not unlike Kant's categories. The notion of innate structures of the human brain naturally implies that there are likely to be innate structures concerning speech and languages, together with the capacity both to speak and to apprehend the meaning of speech. The sense of categorial distinction is certainly innate and pertains to the 'whole animal world'; without it, the survival of separate species would not be possible. Man is part of the animal world, and he is man as part of a group or society and of history. The other, far from being Hell, as Sartre put it, is the only way man has of being aware of himself as man, and this awareness is possible only through language basic to thought, to consciousness, and therefore to being.

Symbolic thought requires language, and for Lévi-Strauss, the basis of human exchanges and that of symbolic thought and of the beginning of culture lies in the uniquely human phenomenon that a man is able to establish relations with another man by means of the exchange of women. This theory is of course rather debatable, and anthropologists have queried it with a good deal of reasonable ground in their arguments. It does seem, at first sight, extremely reductionist and thus limited. Be that as it may, Lévi-Strauss is much permeated with Jakobson's and Saussure's views, and discriminates between language and speech, language being a system of words, and speech a selection of these words for a given utterance. Language is external to any individual, though only partially so, and above all, a given language is part of the collective consciousness of those who speak it, and also makes possible this collective consciousness. For Lévi-Strauss, what matters is not so much consciousness as the collective subconsciousness of mankind, a kind of Jungian *anima mundi* which weighs heavily on the consciousness of man. He goes further than Jung, and credits this universal, subconscious mind with a kind of autonomy of its own, an autonomy which, alas, has been extended by some over-zealous disciples to language itself. 'We do not therefore claim to show how men think, but how myths think themselves in men without their being aware of it.' (*Le Cru et le Cuit*, Plon, 1964, p. 20) Myths express the unconscious aspect of some natural phenomena, and if we look at them, says Lévi-Strauss, we discover that we can reduce them to a few basic ones capable of interpreting and revealing the subconscious of man.

Lévi-Strauss is a follower of Freud, and for him myths are like dreams; they express the subconscious wishes of men, while the incest taboo is, as for Freud, the corner-stone of social relations. The lesson of these relations lies in myths; they are kinds of coded laws, and to ignore them is to court disaster. The problem is how to know them without decoding them, for the decoding itself is fatal. The Sphinx asks questions which must not be answered, for the answer means death; yet, one cannot know the answer without trying to find it; so, Oedipus is caught up in an impossible dilemma, one of the most masterly of god-made ploys. If he wishes to save his native city from disaster, he must try to answer the Sphinx's question; if he does, as he indeed does, he signs his own death warrant. On the other hand, the Fisher King's land remains waste and waterless because no one, not even Sir Gawain Percival, can ask the right question to elicit an answer that obviously was waiting to be given. One can only conclude that man's life is very difficult, and that he is very lucky indeed if he manages to sail safely between the Charybdis of silence and the Scylla of knowing what to say. This necessary wisdom to survive has taken man through many trials and errors, and millennia of struggles, but Lévi-Strauss believes that though he thinks in terms different from those of modern man, primitive man has, from the beginning, been able to think in concrete terms. His thinking was binary, like Jakobson's linguistics, and starting from this notion, Lévi-Strauss looks upon anthropology as a branch of semiology, and he applies its principles to the social behaviour of human beings. Yet, the truth is that neither linguistics nor, still less, anthropology can be reduced to scientific methods of research, without ignoring or distorting empirical facts.

The notion that the incest taboo is the corner-stone of social life is no more universally true than Freud's Oedipus complex. The exchange of women as a means of communication is for Lévi-Strauss something primary and the most elementary form of exchange. Many very primitive societies, like Pygmies and Bushmen, do not have, according to anthropologists like Edmund Leach, unilineal systems of descent. For Lévi-Strauss, 'marriage rules and kinship systems are a kind of language, that is to say a kind of operation designed to ensure, between individuals and groups, certain types of communication. The fact that the *message* would be constituted by *women of the group who circulate* between clans, lineages or families (and not, as is the case with language itself, by the words of the group circulating between individuals) in no way alters the fact that the phenomenon considered in the two cases is identically the same.' (*Anthropologie Structurale*, Plon, 1958, p. 69) Edmund Leach, in his book on Lévi-Strauss, rightly says that 'there is no such identity. If I give an object into the possession of someone else, I no longer possess it myself. . . . If, on the other hand, I transmit a message to someone else by making a speech utterance, I do not deprive myself of anything at all. I merely share information which I originally possessed, but my listener did not.' (*Lévi-Strauss*, Fontana, Collins, 1970, p. 110) This is in fact Valéry's theory of language as communication, a theory which anticipates the Byzantine explanations of the structuralists who talk about the meaning of the word lying in the erasure left by it. Edmund Leach's criticism is perfectly valid, as are most of the admirable and penetrating comments he makes about Lévi-Strauss's various sleights of hand, glossings over of facts and displays of intellectual brilliance which at times obscure rather unsteady arguments.

Lévi-Strauss aims at discovering the evidence for structures that express the truth of the human mind, and here he comes into line with Rousseau, by saying that what is universally true must be natural. This contradicts his previous opposition between nature and culture and his definition of man as non-natural, so that one is faced with one of Lévi-Strauss's paradoxes : in what way is culture, as part of the concept of humanity, distinguishable from nature to which man necessarily belongs? The paradox cannot be solved, for structures cannot be universally true without being grounded in some kind of nature of which man is part. Still, Lévi-Strauss is undeterred by this difficulty, and adopting Freudian terminology, he assimilates the unconscious *id* to nature, and the conscious *ego* to culture. What he calls the human mind is obviously the unconscious mind, and the charting and discovery of this unconscious mind is pursued, not as with Freud, through psychology, but through linguistics, through Jakobson's binary system which is undeniably limited in scope, for it is obviously too rudimentary to explain the complexities of the workings of the mind.

Man is admittedly distinguished from the animal world by language which enables him both to think and to communicate with his fellow beings. Animals also can communicate with one another and with man, through signs, rituals and non-verbal sounds. Man's language goes beyond that and has the capacity to associate the most complex sounds and ideas, to store them up and to recover and transmit them. Whether he communicates or thinks, the concept of man is conceivable as man only in relation with other men, in groups or societies, and therefore both thinking and communication are related to the group or the society to which the thinker or speaker belongs. Thought can transcend both group and society, and reach the universal, the level of historical man in time, for thought is concerned with ideas inherent in man as a social being, irrespective of the society and the time to which he may belong or the language he uses.

But thinking through words is merely analogical to thinking through things, and an analogy remains an analogy. Irrespective of what Lévi-Strauss asserts, primitive man's thinking, performed through things, is different from thinking through words and through concepts and ideas. The first form of thinking is guided by affectivity which has its own logic, its own coherence or structure, but it is not the logic of conceptual thinking which makes possible abstract thought, inductions, deductions, generalisations, articulations and patterns which can only be performed through words as signs and symbols of mental realities. Things are particulars, and they can be used for aesthetic, ethical or religious constructs, but as they have not been conceptualised and categorised, they cannot participate in the construction of mental models. They can be used as direct means of communication, as signs to convey meanings, but they cannot be used as means to communicate the conceptual relationship of things among themselves, or of men with the universe, or to create and store up the knowledge that constitutes the inheritance of a linguistic group or society.

Language, of course, is not only used as a means of communication or as the instrument of thought, but also as the means of creating symbolic entities that convey poetic experience and wisdom. 'We are led to ask ourselves whether various aspects of social life (art, religion) are not phenomena the nature of which rejoins that of language.' (*Anthropologie Structurale*, p. 71) There is indeed a very close relationship between art, religion and language, for they are part of culture, and language and culture are indissociable, they form one single activity, without nevertheless being one and the same thing. A society necessarily implies a language, but a society cannot be absolutely interpreted in terms of language or linguistic rules, and this is the mistake made by some believers in linguistics, beginning with Lévi-Strauss himself, who seems not to be absolutely sure of his beliefs when he says: 'The systems of relationships offer the anthropologist a privileged ground on which his efforts could nearly (and we insist on the word "nearly") rejoin those of the most developed social science, that is to say linguistics.' (*Ibid.*, p. 62)

For Lévi-Strauss the problem of a society is to ensure the

circulation and exchange of women and to replace, through this communication, blood relationship by social relationship. Women, being means of communication, are therefore values, and Lévi-Strauss 'accepts the postulate that there exists a formal correspondence between the structure of language and that of this system of relationships.' (*Ibid.*, p. 72) He accepts this postulate, but he does not attempt to verify it, for, as he himself acknowledges, the attempt is 'extremely precarious', to say the least, and he therefore leaves the burden of verification to others. What fascinates him is what fascinates our science-obsessed age—the urge to reduce all aspects of life to scientific measurements. 'Of all social problems, language alone seems today liable to be submitted to truly scientific studies.' (*Ibid.*, p. 66) Language is therefore the model for his structural analysis. 'The object of comparative structural analysis is neither the French nor the English language, but a certain number of structures which the linguist can reach by starting from an empirical basis such as the phonological structure of French.' (*Ibid.*, p. 98) Other basic social structures such as politeness, cooking, etc., could also be used, and Lévi-Strauss takes his examples from French and English cooking, something that is entertaining but not quite convincing, for reality cannot be easily reduced to the binary forms that he seeks to impose upon it.

Whether in the field of psychology, sociology, linguistics or history, the human element cannot quite be reduced to scientific norms; there is always a residuum of uniqueness which does not fit the abstractions and generalisations in which the scientist would like to enclose it. The human being is thus difficult to handle; the best solution, of course, is to suppress him, or to declare that he no longer exists. In this way, science could really take over and work out theories that no human element could contradict. Thus Lévi-Strauss, who says: 'We believe that the final goal of human sciences is not to constitute man, but to dissolve him.' (*La Pensée Sauvage*, Plon, 1962, p. 326) The means by which this dissolution of man can be attained are not difficult: first, one resorbs particular humanity into general humanity; after that, one reintegrates culture into nature, and finally life back into its physico-chemical conditions. As in the playing of a film backwards, one goes from the omelette back to the egg, or even to the original embryo of the egg. In fact, one plays at being God, even though God has been declared dead, and one goes back and forth at will, along the phylum of creation, from its highest level to its foundations, and why not? —since, as Lévi-Strauss says, 'the essence of savage thought is to be non-temporal. It attempts to apprehend the world at one and the same time as a synchronic and diachronic totality, and the knowledge it has of it resembles that which is offered by a room full of mirrors, one reflecting the other together with the objects that separate them, without being rigorously parallel.' (*Ibid.*, p. 348) This epistemological priority of the synchronic over the diachronic is, admittedly, applicable to primitive societies, but not to history. Lévi-Strauss's anti-humanism is an anti-historicism opposed to the Hegelian and Marxist conception of history. It is a refusal to look upon man as an historical being, and this is an untenable notion, for anthropology necessarily connects with history. Culture cannot be resorbed into nature. The good savage may have existed, but he will not return; what is done cannot be undone. Culture cannot reach a state of primeval nature, it can only reach a state of harmony with nature, in the sense that men will find in it a climate in which knowledge has become a new type of innocence, a means of reconciling men in a truly human society.

So much for structuralism and anthropology. Let us now see some aspects of structuralism in relation to language and literature. The first point to note is that in spite of the attempt to treat language as perfectly conforming to scientific laws, all languages, in spite of some universal characteristics, are the results and the means of communication of ethnic and social groups, and their structures cannot be reduced to one system. Language is part of being, inherent in being and in its evolutive complexification and progression towards self-knowledge. Things are, but do not carry with them the sign by which they are described. This task of description, and therefore of mental organisation of things, is left to man as apex of the evolutionary process. In man lies imprinted the possibility of knowing and categorising the structures that underlie the working and being of creation. There cannot be any universal grammar valid for all languages because grammar is always evolved by individuals who speak and write one, two or three languages, but not a universal language.

Language, either spoken or written, always carries with it an umbilical cord which connects it with the speaker or reader who, using words taken from the common store, always colours them with the strains of his own affectivity and psychic structures. Language, therefore, is never an object, out there to be used by a subject; it is always a subjectivised object, which bears the imprint of its user. The speaker or writer, groping for a meaning to express or to make up in his mind, chooses words according to the glimmering vision of what he is groping for, but he knows perfectly well that the meaning he is looking for, the formulation he will reach, is not, by any stretch of the imagination, some kind of ideal entity lying on the shelves of the universal mind or in Plato's ideal world. There are no such ideal meanings and formulations, except in mathematics; linguistic meanings and formulations are always individual approximations of the ungraspable, final truth. This unavoidable subjectivity of the uses of language does not however make it possible to look upon a given text, or a poem, as a pattern of words, a kind of gossamer through which everyone can contemplate his own dreams and read his own interpretation of nature and experience. The words one reads are not only coloured by the mind and heart of the reader, but they also necessarily carry with them the marks of the affectivity and the mind of whoever it was who put them in the order in which the reader finds them; they have been put in that order, not at random, as if a hundred monkeys had been banging for hours or years on a typewriter, but in an order that aims at the knowledge and expression of a singular thought-emotion experience or truth. The reader follows the text in the way in which a flame follows a stretch of burning cordite : each word ignites the next, so that a continuous flame runs from word to word, right to the end, illuminating the reader's mind, who, through this light, makes up his own experience of the reading which, once completed, will become an unforgettable part of his ethos. However much one may be caught in the wind of dehumanisation, one must face the fact that language, literature and history are unavoidably human activities, and that the ostrich's head in the sand does not stop the desert wind. Fashions and fads may be indulged in, but history as archaeology *à la* Michel Foucault, or criticism *à la* Barthes and others, are notions practically as variable as the changing length of women's skirts.

The notion of man as distinct from the animal implies an innate aptitude for language, but for language as being progressively evolved by man as part of his evolving consciousness. Language is therefore part of the virtualities of being, it is a human process through which man, as a social being, discovers his own meaning and that of the world. It is obvious that consciousness is not dissociable from language, that is to say, language as a body of signs and concepts making it possible to replace the phenomenal world, the presence of others and the feelings and thoughts that one may experience, by signs or mental representations. One could not experience the other without such mental representations which make it possible to experience oneself as experiencing the other, therefore to know oneself through knowing the other, or the presence of the other. So that one never knows oneself as oneself, but always as oneself also knowing others, and in relation with others and with the world in which one lives. Consciousness of one's own existence is also consciousness of the world to which one belongs. The world exists as a mental representation through man's consciousness, and this consciousness comprises both individual and universal structures that shape its apprehension of the phenomenal world, so that man never records photographically, but always modifies or interprets the world, according to his own structures, which are, in varying degrees, according to the lesser or greater range of his genius or talents, in harmony with the structures of nature and the society to which he belongs.

To perceive is to distort, to impose a shape, a style, a conscious and subconscious pattern of values on the world which thus becomes the world of the perceiver, and not everybody else's world. This distortion of the perception of the world continues throughout a whole lifetime, so as to construct, according to whether the perceiver is a philosopher or an artist, a coherent, logical system or a coherent artistic entity or equivalence of the world. That is why painters seem to go on repeating over and over again the same inner structures with different phenomenal appearances; they merely externalise, through their paintings, the essences of their selves combined with the essence of the phenomenal world which they perceive and express. The painter expresses this marriage of essences through colours, volumes and spaces, the poet through words on which he must impose a meaning which, without ignoring the universal meaning each of them has, must connect them, through his inner structure, with the essence of the things that he seeks to recreate symbolically through the written or the spoken word. Language is not self-creative; it is a latency of being, it is a texture of dormant meanings, and it requires the creative mind to awaken these meanings into organic symbolic entities which bear the hall-mark of the mind that brought them to life or that fished them out of the vast subconscious sea—ground of being—to which all human subjectivities can have access in privileged moments of illumination or of perfect detachment from the phenomenal world. Is this sea the Platonic world of ideas, the sea of being, the rational world of Hegel, or Teilhard de Chardin's noosphere? Whatever it is, it is a firmly rooted human notion, the hunting ground of the imagination which draws from it the luminous truths that ceaselessly inspire man's journey towards the accomplishment of his destiny.

For the poet, the truths he offers his fellow-beings are made of words. These words are not objects, bricks or planks in a scientifically shaped building, but living entities made radioactive by the imagination which arrays them together, and they therefore require to be treated as such by the imagination which is going to extract from them the heuristic honey or experience on which it feeds. Therefore man, *anthropos*, whom every prophet of modernity seeks to obliterate, is, on the contrary, very much alive on either side of the tapestry of words which a Penelope artist has woven and another kind of Penelope reader or listener must unweave and reconstruct in his or her own mind. Whatever philosophers or literary mandarins may do or say, they cannot exorcise man from language or from history; they can only express, through such attitudes, subjective, perfectly anthropomorphic notions. *Nouveaux romans, nouveaux nouveaux*

romans, structuralist criticism, all bear the hallmark of the hand-
ful of polar explorers who think that they have left behind them
the fading world of their history and their past, to discover on
the white horizon a pale haze of linguistic structure which is,
according to them, all that remains of the breath and spirit of
Western man. Yet, if they go on walking, they are bound to
discover, beyond the ridges of ice—pure, solipsistic, mental
constructs—green valleys where men still laugh and cry, sing
or tell stories in the shadows of trees as well as chimney stacks,
with the same age-long fears and hopes in their hearts as their
ancestors had, and still going on being, not linguistic emanations,
but living and dying men.

Just as man is not made for the Sabbath, but the Sabbath
is made for man, in the same way language is made for man and
not man for language. Language was already virtually part of
the nebula which preceded the formation of the earth and the
appearance of life upon it; but although the notion of language
is coeval with the notion of man, in the same way as Time is
coeval with Eternity, it nevertheless takes a man, an instrument,
to make possible both mind and language, which embodies his
past, his history and pre-history.

Language is always used individually, literature is always
fragmented in units of varying size, and Mallarmé's dream of
writing *le livre* resolved itself into writing a series of individual
and not negligible books, which, however, could not take the
place of what he would have liked to embody, after his struggle
with the Angel, in the unique summing up or equivalence of
creation called *le livre.* The book as an impersonal, abstract
mirror in which speech, like Narcissus, contemplates its own
intricacies, equilibrium and purely linguistic relationships, is as
impossible as Mallarmé's dream. Language is not a cloak which
the writer puts on, or a garb which he gives to a thought already
formed, it is the instrument through which thought is created.
Thought is not quite coextensive with language, for there are
forms of groping towards expression which one is aware of but
which, in order to be coherent, require to reach linguistic
expression, whether written, spoken or mental. The writer gropes
for thought and knows his thought, and consequently certain
aspects of himself, only once he has found the means of express-

ing or constructing his thought. He is what he thinks and what his readers will endlessly make him, a continuously changing subjectivity modified by other subjectivities, an interpreting, continuously interpreted consciousness which no structuralist notion of objectivity can annihilate.

The structuralist critic would like only to concern himself with the linguistic structure of a given work, and analyse it as linguistic relationships which have to be what they are as if they existed without any reference to the sensibility or the mind that brought together the various Ariadne's threads of this construction. The subject is reduced to zero in literature as well as in history or in psychology. Barthes as well as Foucault and Lacan agree on this point which attempts to do away with any notion of the existence of a Cartesian *cogito*. The subject disappears, dissolves itself and loses its own structure and that of the world in the structure of speech which takes the place of both. But the point that is ignored is that speech does not structure itself according to ceaselessly engendered self-causes, it is structured by a subject consciously or subconsciously aware of the world to which it belongs.

Meaning implies the existence of a subject which gives, and of another which receives and which makes its own meaning. The words of the world, folded up in various dictionaries, asleep or whirling around in men's memories, cannot organise themselves into meaningful linguistic structures, except through the consciousness or the subconsciousness of human beings. Mallarmé's transcendentalism, his abolition or annihilation of reality and its replacement by the poem, was made by the poet's consciousness fused into the poem, which became the transcendental *I*, shining alone between the nothingness engendered by the creative act and the nothingness that encompasses it. Structuralist criticism is even more recondite and ethereal, for if creative writing is, in structuralist terms, speech structuring itself without any intervening consciousness, criticism is speech structuring itself according to speech that has already structured itself, that is to say language as a self-structured emanation, supposedly resting on language as a self-structured emanation, or on what Shakespeare would have called airy nothings, without any poet having given them a local habitation and a name, for the poet has been abolished. Literary activity is thus reduced to the self-organising or structuring of an ontological entity—language—which has become the being of being, and which, like the waves of the sea, endlessly makes and unmakes delightful patterns of foam for the entertainment of the structuralist critic who superimposes on them the patterns of another sea which, unlike the first, is without depth, tides or organic life, and consists only in the ripples of its surface. That is perhaps why Gilles Deleuze can say : 'Structuralism owes nothing to Albert Camus, but a lot to Lewis Carroll. . . . The manifesto of structuralism ought to be looked for in the eminently poetic, theatrical and famous formula—thinking is a throw of the dice.' (*Histoire de la Philosophie*, ed. F. Châtelet, vol. 8, *Le XXe Siècle*, Hachette, 1973, p. 307)

Roland Barthes is the best known representative of structuralism in literature and literary criticism. Lacan, Foucault and Althusser are the other names generally associated with this new ideology. Jacques Lacan is the fashionable psychoanalyst, and he is supposed to have done for Freud what Althusser is supposed to have done for Marx, that is to say rejuvenated him, adapted him to contemporary thought—one could say stretched him, in spite of his protests, on the Procrustean bed of structuralism to bring him up to date. The up-to-daters always proceed in such fashion, and woe to the one they choose ! It will probably take a long time for him to recover from this kind of surgery. Freud's scientism has been given yet an extra dose of scientism by Lacan who, applying linguistic theories and measurements to the subconscious, has produced a new chart of the world of dreams and desires which Freud, had he been able to decode its linguistic signs, would have perhaps turned into another wonderful Eastern journey made by a new Marco Polo.

For Lacan, the subconscious is not the secret world of repressed instincts, but the source of speech, and if one applies to it the rules of structuralist linguistics, the mystery can be unravelled, for speech is not the expression of a speaking subject, but an emergence from the subconscious, constituting a subject that finds its fulfilment in intersubjectivity or harmony with other subjects. The notion of subject, generally banned from literary structuralism, here becomes nevertheless necessary, for a speech must have a listener—the analyst—and speech itself emerges through a subject who, thanks to it, knows himself in part, and is helped to find his equilibrium in time through the mediation of the listening and catalysing analyst. There is, therefore, in Lacan's theories a humanism which is alien to structuralism, but his attempt to assess the subconscious and its symbolism through linguistic laws is patently untenable, for it posits an order of pre-eminence between two aspects of the human psyche that is by definition contradictory, for the turgid world of the subconscious necessarily precedes and underlies language and linguistic structurations which are not universal. The subconscious, according to Lacan, is structured like a language. Yet the individual subconscious can never be known as such. It can only be partially known through conscious thought, speech, actions or representations, but it never makes itself completely known. There always remains a residuum of non-knowledge, a lack or absence which is different with every individual. So that one cannot equate the subconscious with speech or language in order to grant pre-eminence or primacy to the former. 'The subconscious,' says Lévi-Strauss, 'is always empty, consisting only in the structural laws that it imposes upon representations as well as upon desires.' (*Anthropologie Structurale*, p. 224) Knowledge, whether derived from experience or intuition, is always individual, and speech and language are always connected with the human element, and they can never be either deified or reified.

Michel Foucault's anti-humanism is neither that of Lévi-Strauss nor that of Althusser, though it is extremely close to them, for following Lévi-Strauss, he endeavours to apply scientific method to the study of history. He too is in search of structures that he calls *épistémè*,* and he applies the archaeological method, the study of the substrata of history, to history itself. He is looking for the genealogies of historical changes, and the clue lies in language, for language is the only objective structured

---

* 'The aim of this study is to bring to light the epistemological field, the *épistémè*, in which knowledge, leaving aside all criteria concerning its rational value or its objective forms, grounds its positivity and exhibits thus a history which is not that of its growing perfection, but rather that of its conditions of possibility; this essay should bring out the structures which have given rise to the various forms of empirical knowledge.' Michel Foucault, *Les Mots et les Choses*, Gallimard, 1966, p. 13.

reality. Nietzsche had announced the death of God and the coming of the superman—Nietzsche himself. A hundred years later we have the death of man, and the emergence of the notion of the existence of language from which the subject is excluded. 'The being of language,' says Foucault, 'only appears with the disappearance of the subject.' (In *Critique*, June 1966) The outcome of this is the establishment, in various aspects of culture, of an irreconcilable incompatibility between the being of language and the existence of an individual consciousness. The experience of this incompatibility makes itself clear in the act of writing, in attempts to formalise language, in the study of myths and psychoanalysis, and in the search for a *logos* which could be the basis of the whole of Western rationalism.

The *épistémè* of a given period is its structure or the quasi-transcendental pattern of objective categories which determine the various cycles of knowledge. Each *épistémè* favours or makes possible certain scientific developments and forms of knowledge, and precludes others. The main tendency of this approach to history is to construct closed, separate fields, and to avoid progressive developments and transformations. The boundaries of these fields are necessarily arbitrary, and the same arbitrariness necessarily applies to the epistemological conclusion drawn from such compartmentalisations. Marxism, deprived of its true economic and social infrastructures, is made to appear as meaningless, and all its manifestations from 1848 to the Russian revolution, as well as Mao's long march and the Vietnam war, lose their economic infrastructures and appear as empty agitations and games, for according to such a reading of history the *épistémè* in which Marx was born was disappearing and already belonged to archaeology. So history is absurd and perhaps a new history will have to be born; the Nietzschean superman will only rise from the ashes of man. 'Modern political thought does not formulate any ethics, in as far as any imperative is part of thought and of its movement to apprehend non-thought. . . . In truth, modern thought has never been able to propose an ethic. The reason for this is not that it is pure speculation, but on the contrary that it is, from the start, and in itself, a mode of action.' (Michel Foucault, *Les Mots et les Choses*, p. 339)

Louis Althusser has sought to rejuvenate Marxism in the light of structuralism, and he has begun by denying or ignoring the existence of Marx's humanism and historicism. 'Speaking strictly of theory, one can and one must speak openly of a theoretical Marxist anti-humanism and see in this theoretical anti-humanism the absolute condition of the positive knowledge of the human world and its transformations. One can only do something about man on the absolute condition of reducing to ashes the philosophical myth of man.' (*Pour Marx*, Maspero, 1966, p. 236) This echoes Lévi-Strauss's call which is: 'We believe that the final goal of human sciences is not to constitute man but to dissolve him.' (*La Pensée Sauvage*, p. 326) Lukács, whose claims to being the most eminent commentator on Marx are difficult to disregard, says: 'Marxism is separated from bourgeois sociology, milieu-theories, etc. not only by its radical criticism of society and historicism, but also by the recognition of this dialectic unity of individual and society: it is human activity that shapes society and the objective motion of society can only be realised through individuals. It is as a social being that man could become a human individual, and not stay a mere natural entity.' (Preface to *Art and Society*, 1967, reproduced in *The New Hungarian Quarterly*, XIII, 47, Autumn 1972, pp. 55–56)

Althusser's Marxism seems to me both a contradiction in terms and an anachronism. It is a contradiction in terms because it claims to be both Marxism and pure scientific theory, while Marxism is above all knowledge and praxis. It is an anachronism because the so-called structural foundation of Marxism which Althusser posits is a notion that Marxism itself would have refuted as a form of applied essentialism or idealism, alien to its pragmatic and existential basis. Neither Lévi-Strauss, who dreams of man's dissolution, nor Foucault, who proclaims the death of man, has set himself the aim of discovering the ideal structure of social and economic evolution. Just like Jan Kott, who seems to have thought that Shakespeare did not quite understand what he was doing and only wrote *Lear* and *Hamlet* to be part of the black pessismism of the theatre of cruelty that he, Kott, was going to propound, Althusser claims that Marx did not quite know what he was doing, but that he was a structuralist without knowing it. Althusser claims, wrongly of course, that philosophy always follows scientific knowledge and that therefore the philosophy of Marxism could only be written not by Marx himself, but by those who came after him, like Lenin, or Althusser himself. In *Lénine et la Philosophie* (Maspero, 1972, p. 22) he says: 'that is why philosophy, in the strict sense, began only with Plato', ignoring therefore Pythagoras, Heraclitus and many others, both mathematicians and philosophers, from whom Plato derived a great deal of his philosophical system, to say nothing of Eastern thought which did not carry with it, like early Greek thought, any scientific interpretation of the universe.

What a singular notion Althusser propounds, when he claims that 'philosophy arises only once the evening has fallen, once science, born at dawn, has already covered the span of a day.* With regard to science which causes its birth in its pristine form, and its rebirth in its revolutions, philosophy has always been a full day behind, a day which can last years, twenty years, half a century or a century.' (*Ibid.*, p. 23) Needless to say, this statement is not supported by evidence. It ignores the fact that, for instance, Newton and Leibniz were not only contemporaries but controversialists on topics about which, together with their friends, they did not quite see eye to eye. They were both deeply permeated with Cartesianism which played a part in their respective fields. Leibniz and Descartes were both philosophers and mathematicians, and Leibniz, with his discovery of infinitesimal calculus, bridges the gap between East and West, and is a crucial figure in science as well as philosophy. 'The time was not ready,' says Althusser, 'the evening had not yet fallen, and neither Marx nor Engels nor Lenin could write the great philosophical work which Marxism lacked.' (*Ibid.*, p. 25) Well, now it is done, and although Lukács and Gramsci tried, they have obviously failed, continuing to look upon Marxism as a post-Hegelian philosophy of praxis. The various worker movements also failed because of their theoretical deviations called evolutionism, humanism, empiricism, etc., but now, light is on the horizon, and all these failures by men who happen to have been born too early, before the moment for the true philosophical interpretation was ripe, will be made good, and from the empyrean they will witness, at last, the triumph of truly understood Marxism!

* Althusser cannot be speaking here of philosophy in general, but only of the philosophy of science.

Even Lenin was born too early, or, as Althusser suggests, Lenin's philosophy is not quite philosophy, because the 'game' that he played in philosophy is not quite philosophy. Just as well, for Lenin had not only clearly said that philosophy is not science —a very non-structuralist proposition—but also that 'one cannot perfectly understand Karl Marx's *Capital*, and in particular its first chapter, without having exhaustively studied and understood the whole of Hegel's logic. Therefore not a single Marxist for half a century after him has understood Marx.' (*Ibid.*, p. 78) These are very serious stumbling blocks on the path to the structuralisation of Marxism; Hegel is indeed the bugbear of Marxist structuralism, and if philosophy cannot be made into a science, where does Marxist structuralism stand? Althusser seems to get over these problems. 'Philosophy is distinct from science,' says Lenin, 'its categories are distinct from scientific concepts'; yet the philosophical concept of structure is, as we shall see, given the status of a scientific concept. Words are certainly interchangeable, but their attributes are not; a philosophical concept is neither factually verifiable nor falsifiable; a scientific concept should be both, yet *Capital* is not a scientific analysis and statement of possible remedies, but a treatise of political economy, resting upon major concepts based on facts, but certainly not all scientifically verifiable.

A structure is, as has been pointed out, a whole or a model in which the parts cohere, so as to create an originality and a specificity that can only be understood as emanating from the relationship of the one part to the other, and its wholeness as resting upon the law or cause that holds them all together. This is the model or basic structure that makes possible the scientific interpretation not of history, but of histories, for history as such, with its diachronic unfolding and continuity towards a Christian, Hegelian or Marxist finality, is repudiated. Every structure is part of a self-contained field, which can be political, sociological, ideological, philosophical, scientific, etc., with its own synchronic time, obviously difficult to relate to any diachronic notion of wholeness or perenniality, invariance or *Zeitgeist* emanating from the dialectical interplay of evolutionary forces at work in history as they are at work in biology, culture, and other aspects of life. There is no doubt that the structure of production influences society, though it is certainly less important than the labour-power and the labour-value relationships. A structuralist theory of production is not possible because economics is not pure mathematics, and its values are not fixed and of universal value, but arguable and changing according to the situation and the political and ideological climate of the moment and place. A structuralist theory of production is not applicable to a whole nation. It is bound to vary from one social group to another, from one geographical area to another, and from one type of production to another. There is no possibility of scientific standardisation, and one is thus confronted with a complex of autonomous synchronic models, which the checkmaster handles according to his affectivity and ideology. The concept of a fixed structure of production which is a transposition of Platonism or Spinozism to sociology and to the philosophy of history, is a form of theoretical abstract thinking about differential relationships between symbolic objects and agents, that ignores the complexity of the human reality which does not conform to any fixed model, Platonic, Spinozist or otherwise, but which changes according to the interplay of the variables, virtualities and circumstances that are the component elements of the evolution of man and history.

One cannot create a philosophy by starting from methods and ideas applicable to a given domain only. One can use these methods and ideas as an epistemological basis in order to assess the value of these very methods and ideas, but this is a purely tautological operation of no other value except as a closed mental performance disconnected from existential reality. Historical materialism rests upon dialectical materialism which illumines the relationship between the phenomenal object and the object of thought, and it can be tested only against changing facts and not against any structure or model of production—part of scientific mythology.

Althusser denies the existence of the humanism and historicism of Marxism on the grounds of a complete cleavage or epistemological gap between the Marx of the German ideology and various early writings and notes, and *Capital*. The notion that there are two Marxes, that the author of *Capital* is completely different from the Marx of the 1840s and 1850s, is difficult to maintain in theory as well as in the domain of factual evidence.

Marx is neither an artist, who changes his style through life, nor a natural scientist, who discovers new aspects of truth; he is a philosopher and an economist, and as such there is an organic wholeness in his life and work, and he would be a very singular philosophical hybrid if he were fish in youth and flesh in later life. His thought certainly matured according to his experience and to the changing socio-historical context in which he developed, but his Kantian apparatus of categories merely evolved with him; he did not acquire a new one in middle age. Althusser can only dispose of Marx's humanism by ignoring, in his reading of *Capital*, all references to man, to the part played by the proletariat and revolutionary praxis, to Hegel's influence and to Marx's deeply human Messianism, in order to conform to his preconceived structuralist anti-humanism and his pseudo-scientific notion of synchronic, non-diachronic structures. This attempt to look upon history *sub specie aeternitatis* ignores the diachronic unfolding of social thinking through Fourier, Proudhon, Ricardo and Marx, and its no less diachronic and very concrete application with Lenin, Stalin, Khrushchev or Mao. This synchronic epistemology is part of the process of the dehumanisation of man, and the replacement of the role of individual or group consciousness by that of so-called masses, and by scientific models or structures through which one can read the truth about mankind as one reads the truth of mathematical laws through algebraic equations. This is part of the dominant obsession with science; it ignores the fire and the mire of history which is not shaped by abstractions, but according to the vagaries of the mind and those of 'the foul rag-and-bone shop of the heart'.

The dialectical interplay between man and language and society and language, is boldly reduced by structuralist theorists to language, that is to say to a form of positivistic materialism and literary positivism. Truth has become a matter of technological achievement and computerised assessments in which empirico-positivistic cognition treats all aspects of physical and mental life as phenomena perfectly amenable to the logic of science which reduces being to its phenomenality. This approach to life and to knowledge leaves no room for philosophy except as epistemology dominated by scientific criteria of verifiability, falsifiability, systematic clarity and circular hermeneutics. This scientific positivism which explains God as an anthropomorphic notion, in order to allay man's fears, uses a similar process in order to protect itself against the opacity and mystery that are still part of life; it declares them out of bounds, as being beyond positivistic measurements, and therefore part of the uncharted domain of metaphysics. It ignores the fact that from Anaximander to Pythagoras, Descartes, Newton or Einstein, men of science as well as philosophers have never confused their scientific researches with their metaphysical preoccupations. Modern man is well aware of the importance of science, yet he cannot turn it into a religion and into the basis and criterion of all human values. Empirico-scientific truth, important though it is, is not the whole human truth, and in the realm of philosophy and literature no solution can be hoped for by transferring the ontological argument from metaphysics to linguistics and making of language the being of Being.

The notion of God as the Feuerbachian recipient of man's alienation has died a natural death. Man's growing consciousness of his own importance in creation has made of Him a participant in this creation, and no longer a guide, a judge or a dispenser of values. As for man himself, the incarnation of being, informed with Being, he is neither dead nor replaced by language as the link between Being and being. He is more and more aware of his responsibilities. He is aware that the speculations of reason must be grounded in the negativities of existence. He is aware that these negativities must not be rejected or objectified into a form of nihilism that then paralyses existence to the point of making it constantly oscillate between materialistic sensualism and flights into a world of dreams or illusory heavens. The negative aspects of life are part of the continuous evolution of values, of the interplay between the infinite virtualities of existence which represent the element of chance, and the invariables of creation and life which necessarily assume and absorb what they need, and reject the unused or used-up as non-being, which is the lining of being.

The French intelligentsia, not to be confused with French creative writers—novelists, poets and philosophers—but comprising above all avant-gardists, grammarians, philosopher-commentators and some literary critics, is intent upon reducing all types of writing to linguistic systems, and all systems to one single master system, the key to all systems. Like walkers in a wood, entranced by the dew-laden, spider's web traceries that capture their gaze, they forget the fact that there is somewhere a spider which has done the work. They forget the fact that *l'écriture* and *la parole* require a human consciousness, and that Racine can no more be explained by organigrams than Baudelaire's poetry can be assessed by scientific measurements. They overlook the illogicality of the so-called opposition between *parole* or speech and *écriture* or writing, speech being in their view the only means of realising a presence and a presentation of living truth. They forget the fact that, in Western civilisation, writing is basically, at least in its Greek origins, the transcription of speech, and science and philosophy partook of its dialectical structures and logic, without neglecting, of course, Platonism and neo-Platonism and the intuitionism and mysticism of the East which make themselves felt more and more through Leibniz, Hegel, Schopenhauer, Bergson and others. Plato, Socrates and Christ were, no doubt, representatives of an oral civilisation, yet we know their words only because someone wrote them down, and because Plato did so both for himself and for his master Socrates. He did what most poets, philosophers and statesmen do, he wrote down what he said, and he may even, as in most cases, have written down what he said before he said it. The *logos*, God's incarnation in being, is both one and multiple, and speech and language are as much parts of its connection with Being, as the transcendental silence that merges being into Being. Rembrandt's famous painting of St Paul writing under the impact of Divine inspiration makes it clear that speech and writing are two forms of expression that are not opposed, but are two ways of conveying the same wisdom or experience. Jean-Jacques Rousseau, who desperately wanted to expose his inner self, or at least what he thought to be his inner self, to others and to posterity, realised that he could achieve this aim only through writing, and not through preaching at street corners or in lecture halls.

Michel Foucault, in his polemic with Jacques Derrida about

Descartes, admirably sums up the Byzantinism and the barren-
ness of the type of intellectualism that prevails now in thought
and the arts, when he says : 'I shall not say that it is metaphysics,
or its end, which lies behind this "textualisation" of discursive
practices. I shall go much further : I shall say that it is a minor
pedagogy, historically well determined and which in a very
visible way manifests itself. It is a pedagogy that teaches the
pupil that there is nothing beyond the text . . . that it is therefore
not necessary to look elsewhere, except in it, and not of course
in the words, but in the words as erasures, as part of a code, and
that it is only here that one can find "the meaning of being".
It is a pedagogy which, on the other hand, gives the voice of the
master the boundless sovereignty which makes it possible for him
to repeat the text endlessly.' (*Histoire de la Folie*, 'Bibliothèque
des Histoires', Gallimard, 1972, Appendix p. 602) The meaning of a word obviously cannot lie in the erasure that
it leaves behind; it is bound to lie in the semantic and
syntactical radiations as apprehended by an individual consciousness which constructs from it its own duration and
experience.

The so-called notion of demolishing metaphysics from the
inside is like Samson pulling down the temple on his head. First
of all, there has to be a temple to pull down, and for the moment
there is no such thing; there are only scavengers looking for
ruins. There is no such thing as overcoming or overthrowing
metaphysics, neither from the inside nor from the outside, for
metaphysics is an interpretation of Being by beings and therefore
an attempt, by being, to discover or to apprehend the Being of
beings. The total apprehension or knowledge of Being is neither
attainable nor desirable, for it could only lead to a confrontation
with the terror of the void. But the fact to remember is that
Being or truth, for the two are one, can be approached only
through individuated being, therefore philosophy in as far as it
is concerned with Being is bound to remain humanistic and
metaphysical. Mystical experience may precede the verbal
revelation of truth, or the light of truth may be such, as is
the case at the end of *The Divine Comedy*, that it reduces being
to total silence and to its enfolding into Being, but truth as a
manifestation of Being can come to men only through language

used as the medium of thought, for there cannot be any thought without language.

Language gives man the true essence of his humanity; that is why language cannot be conceived of as a self-created entity or as an emanation of Being, without any beings to receive it. Least of all could one look upon language as a universal, abstract notion applicable to all men. The notion of a universal language, totalising all possibilities of expression and relations between Being and being, is absurd. As long as the world lasts, there will be possibilities of new expression, and the world will necessarily end before it has been fully expressed. The concept of language is applicable to all men, for it is the concept of language as a means of communication between beings, and between beings and Being, or truth revealing through language the self-knowledge of being.

The attributes that are necessarily part of the concept of language can be implemented only at the existential level, by moving from the notion of one ideal language to a multiplicity of languages, retaining no doubt basic attributes and structures, but expressing the ethnic groups that evolved them and also the social classes and the historical changes that pertain to these groups. Each language is rooted in beings as ethnic or national groups, part of the history of mankind. It is not an ens spontaneously manifesting its grammar and structures through a few chosen individuals, but a means by which singular individuals can reveal or communicate to their fellow beings the truth or essence of the human situation, both at an historical, lived moment and at the perennial level of history and truth valid for all time. It is also a means of everyday communication between human beings; but whatever the level at which it is used—poetry as revelation of truth, prose as creative experience and wisdom in novels and philosophy, or everyday utterance—it always requires individual consciousness.

In Conclusion

One cannot sum up three generations of philosophical speculations in a few sentences, and one can even less attempt to
prophesy what tomorrow might bring. This book is neither a
history of philosophy in France during the last seventy years nor
a philosophical chronicle of that period. Either attempt would
require volumes. The main aim of this study has been confined
to examining and assessing the most important aspects of French
thought during the period mentioned, focusing on the most
intrinsically important thinkers and on those whose socio-
historical impact could not be ignored. If, for instance, thinkers
like Blondel, Jean Wahl or Mounier have not been discussed,
it is simply because Bergson or Marcel have covered the same
ground, and gone further. At the end of this period one is
compelled to note that attempts at the establishment of philosophical systems or at doctrinal philosophy are definitely at an
end. Why it should be so is difficult to say. Society, Western
society at least, repudiates systems, hierarchies, established moral
canons and doctrines, and from political to aesthetic, moral and
religious dogmas, throws everything into the melting-pot of
re-examination. The dominant attitude of the moment is an
attitude of revolt, negation to the point of nihilism, and ceaseless
questioning. Art and thought correspond to this attitude, and
philosophical writings, whatever they may be, are above all
critical and exploratory of texts and of language. The text is
all, and individual consciousness, history and praxis leave the
stage to words about words, and to purely abstract, dehumanised
notions or systems. Thus Althusser on Marxism and Lacan on
Freud. The theoretician talks about theory, and by so doing
builds a theory from which it follows that the most important

188

aspects of thought and life are the theoretician and the theory that explains all. This is, as we have seen, the corner-stone of structuralism.

Philosophic thought, what there is of it, is fragmented and fractious, whether in politics or in psychology and psycho-analysis; it is the product of conflicting groups. The Freudian bible is subject to as many interpretations as the Bible itself, and the result is worse, for the various interpretations are all carried out in the name of a fierce positivism which seeks to use facts to support social or aesthetic attitudes. Science itself is infected with politics, and its past associations with capitalism and bourgeois society have not been cleansed by a hundred years of so-called scientific Marxism or by notions of pseudo-scientific objectivity. Science, like everything else, is found to be stained by the human. Scientists are not gods, and there is no possibility of establishing an Olympian epistemology as valid for all as mathematical principles.

In our time there is nothing to worship, nothing to respect without questioning; though there is, of course, transcendence for those—and they are numerous—who still believe in it; but these people are not vocal, and they are not agitating or pub-lishing manifestoes, therefore their silence is equated with non-existence. As irreverence and questioning are common attributes of youth, the young naturally tend to believe that the world is centred upon Althusser, Lacan, Foucault and Derrida. Such oversimplification is one of the natural dangers encountered by any attempt to assess a contemporary scene while one is part of it; for one hears or sees only those who shout or agitate, while those who think or work silently remain unnoticed. Yet in most cases it is the latter who represent the real structures of social life and thought, and who maintain the movement which is the essence of life.

We are, it seems to me, in a phase of purely verbal philoso-phising, just as politics is above all verbal and visual—constant material for films or tele-reporting. A seismic, iconoclastic tremor shakes the world, and age-old statues in philosophic and religious buildings tumble down, their foundations having finally been disintegrated by ceaseless positivistic analyses, while restless youth, and some anarchic elements which are the necessary froth of dogmatic societies, fill the front of the stage with their words and their actions. The dialectics between order and disorder, that is to say between the increasing dogmatism of rock-like states and the eroding tides of analyses, irreverence and search for novelty, are bound to go on, until some form of equilibrium is reached which reconciles the revolutionary, peripheral forces of modern society with the bureaucratic, authoritarian forces that, all over the world, oppose them. Philosophical discourse, which used to rest upon reason and logic, is now fragmented and no longer expository, descriptive or revelatory of the nature of being, but is used as a weapon of demolition so as to bring to life new values or a Nietzschean transvaluation of values. Thence the obsession with language used as an instrument for rejecting philosophy, in a world which is growing more and more opposed to imperial cities, supermen or great avatars of spiritual or political power. The French philosophical stage is practically bare. Sartre's figure fades away in the distance, and the centre stage is dominated by a babel of philosophical discources about philosophical discourse—something strangely reminiscent of the atmosphere of sophistry in Athens before Socrates. One can hear above the hubbub of noise the distinctive voices of Gilles Deleuze, Pierre Klossovski and Michel Foucault, but there is certainly no Socrates or Plato to be discerned in the distance.

BIBLIOGRAPHY

English editions cited are those currently available; many of these are also available in paperback. English editions of French works are given in brackets immediately following details of French editions, the English title being cited only when it differs significantly from the original. The place of publication of all French editions cited is Paris.

General reading

Aron, R., *Introduction à la Philosophie de l'Histoire*, Gallimard, 1938. *La Philosophie critique de l'Histoire*, Vrin, 1964.
Blondel, M., *La Philosophie et l'Esprit chrétien*, Presses Universitaires de France (PUF), 2 vols, 1945, 1949. *L'Action*, Alcan and PUF, 1963.
Bréhier, E., *Les Théories actuelles de la Philosophie contemporaine*, PUF, 1961.
Chevalier, J., *Histoire de la Pensée*, Flammarion, 1955.
Deleuze, G., *Nietzsche et la Philosophie*, PUF, 1962. *La Philosophie critique de Kant*, PUF, 1967.
Duvignaud, J., *Sociologie du Théâtre*, PUF, 1965.
Focillon, H., *Vie des Formes*, PUF, 1970.
Freud, S., *Civilisation and its Discontents*, Norton, New York, 1962; Hogarth Press, London, 1963. *The Future of an Illusion*, Hogarth Press, 1962; Doubleday, New York. *The Interpretation of Dreams*, Basic Books, New York, 1954; Allen & Unwin, London, 1955. *Leonardo da Vinci and a Memory of his Childhood*, Norton, 1964. *Moses and Monotheism*, Hogarth Press, 1951; Random House, New York, 1955. *On Dreams*, Hogarth Press, 1952; Norton, 1962. *The Psychopathology of Everyday Life*, Ernest Benn, London, 1960; Norton, 1971. *Three Essays on the Theory of Sexuality*, Hogarth Press; Basic Books, 1962.

191

Gilson, E., *Le Thomisme*, Paris, 1945.

Grenier, J., *L'Existence*, Gallimard, 1945.

Guitton, J., *Le Génie de Pascal*, Aubier, 1963.

Heidegger, M., *Being and Time*, SCM, London, 1962; Harper & Row, New York, 1962. *Existence and Being*, Vision Press, London, 1949; Regnery, Chicago, 1950. *Héraclite*, Gallimard, 1973. *Kant and the Problem of Metaphysics*, Indiana Univ. Press, Bloomington, Ind., 1962. *The Question of Being*, Twayne, New York, 1958; Vision Press, London, 1959. *What is Philosophy?* Columbia Univ. Press, 1956; Vision Press, London, 1963. *What's Called Thinking?* Harper & Row, New York and London, 1968.

Jaspers, K., *Philosophy is for Everyman*, Harcourt Brace, New York, 1967. *Philosophical Faith and Revelation*, Collins, London, 1971.

Lacroix, J., *Kant et le Kantisme*, PUF, 1969. *Marxisme, Existentialisme, Personnalisme*, PUF, 1970. *Panorama de la Philosophie française contemporaine*, PUF, 1968.

Lalande, A., *La Raison et les Normes*, Vrin, 1963.

Le Senne, R., *Introduction à la Philosophie*, PUF, 1970. *Traité de Morale Générale*, PUF, 1967.

Levinas, E., *La Théorie de l'Intuition dans la Phénoménologie de Husserl*, Alcan, 1963.

Mounier, E., *Le Personnalisme*, PUF, 1946. *Oeuvres*, Le Seuil, 4 vols, 1944–50.

Picon, G. (ed.), *Panorama des Idées contemporaines*, Gallimard, 1957.

Polin, R., *La Création des Valeurs*, PUF, 1952.

Smith, C., *Contemporary French Philosophy*, Methuen, London, 1964.

Tilliette, X., *Philosophie contemporaine*, Desclée de Brouwer, 1962.

Trotignon, P., *Les Philosophes français d'aujourd'hui*, PUF, 1970.

Wahl, J., *Esquisse d'une Histoire de l'Existentialisme*, Paris, 1949. *Philosophies of Existence*, Routledge and Kegan Paul, London, 1954; Schocken, New York.

Works by and about authors studied

Bergson, Henri, *Oeuvres*, PUF, ed. Gouhier, Paris, 1959, containing:
Essai sur les Données Immédiates de la Conscience (1889). *Matière et Mémoire* (1896) (Allen & Unwin, London, 1911;

Humanities Press, New York, 1970). *Le Rire* (1900). *L'Evolution Créatrice* (1907). *L'Energie Spirituelle* (1919). *Les Deux Sources de la Morale et de la Religion* (1932). *La Pensée et le Mouvant* (1934). *Duration and Simultaneity*, Bobbs-Merrill, Indianapolis, Ind., 1965. *Time and Free Will*, Humanities Press, 1971.

Alexander, I., *Bergson*, Bowes & Bowes, Cambridge, 1957.
Barthélémy-Madaule, J., *Bergson et Teilhard de Chardin*, PUF, 1963. *Bergson*, PUF, 1968.
Chevalier, J., *Bergson*, Plon, 1926.
Deleuze, G., *Le Bergsonisme*, PUF, 1965.
Maire, G., *Aux Marches de la Civilisation Occidentale*, La Baudinière, 1929.

Husserl, Edmund, *Cartesian Meditations*, Nijhoff, The Hague, 1960; Humanities Press, New York, 1960. *Ideas*, Macmillan, New York, 1962; Allen & Unwin, London, 1967.
Merleau-Ponty, Maurice, *Les Aventures de la Dialectique*, Gallimard, 1955 (Northwestern University Press, Evanston, Ill., 1973). *Bulletin de Psychologie*, no. 236, November 1964 : Résumé des cours de Merleau-Ponty à la Sorbonne (Themes from the lectures at the Collège de France 1952–60, Northwestern Univ. Press, 1970). *Eloge de la Philosophie*, Gallimard, 1953 (Northwestern Univ. Press, 1963.) *Humanisme et Terreur*, Gallimard, 1947 (Beacon Press, Boston, Mass., 1969). *L'Oeil et l'Esprit*, Gallimard, 1961. *Phénoménologie de la Perception*, Gallimard, 1945 (Humanities Press, New York; Routledge & Kegan Paul, London, 1962). *Prose du Monde*, Gallimard, 1969 (Northwestern Univ. Press, 1973). *Sens et Non-sens*, Nagel, 1948 (Northwestern Univ. Press, 1964). *Signes*, Gallimard, 1960 (Northwestern Univ. Press, 1964). *La Structure du Comportement*, PUF, 1942 (Beacon Press, 1963). *Le Visible et l'Invisible*, Gallimard, 1963 (Northwestern Univ. Press, 1969).

Hyppolite, J., *Existence et Dialectique dans la Philosophie de Merleau-Ponty*, *Les Temps Modernes*, nos. 184–185, June 1961.
Ricoeur, P., *Hommage à Merleau-Ponty*, *Esprit*, June 1961.
Sartre, J.-P., *Merleau-Ponty*, *Situations V*, Gallimard.

Sartre, Jean-Paul, *L'Imagination*, PUF, 1936. *L'Imaginaire: psychologie phénoménologique de l'imagination*, Gallimard, 1940 (*The Psychology of Imagination*, Rider, London, 1949; Washington Square Press, New York). *L'Etre et le Néant: essai d'ontologie phénoménologique*, Gallimard, 1943 (*Being and Nothingness*, Philosophical Library, New York, 1956; Methuen, London, 1957). *L'Existentialisme est un Humanisme*, Nagel, 1946 (Philosophical Library, New York, 1947; Methuen, London, 1948). *Réflexions sur la Question Juive*, Morihien, 1946 (*Portrait of the Anti-Semite*, Secker & Warburg, London, 1948; *Anti-Semite and Jew*, Schocken, New York, 1948). *Baudelaire*, Gallimard, 1947 (Horizon, London, 1949; New Directions, New York, 1950). *Situations I to X*, Gallimard, Paris, 1947–72 (Hamish Hamilton, London; Braziller, New York, 1965). *Saint Genet, comédien et martyr*, Gallimard, Paris, 1952 (Braziller, New York). *Critique de la raison dialectique*, Gallimard, 1960. *Les Mouches*, Gallimard, 1943 (*The Flies*, in *Two Plays*, Hamish Hamilton, London, 1946; *No Exit and the Flies*, Knopf, New York, 1947). *Les Mains sales*, Gallimard, 1948 (*Crime Passionnel*, Methuen, 1961). *Le Diable et le bon Dieu*, Gallimard, 1951 (*Lucifer and the Lord*, Hamish Hamilton, 1953; *The Devil and the Good Lord*, Knopf, 1960). *Les Séquestrés d'Altona*, Gallimard, 1956 (*Loser Wins*, Hamish Hamilton, 1960; *Condemned of Altona*, Knopf, 1961).

Campbell, R., *Jean-Paul Sartre, ou une littérature philosophique*, Ardent, 1945.
Cranston, M., *Sartre*, Oliver & Boyd, Edinburgh and London, 1962.
Greene, N. N., *Jean-Paul Sartre: The Existentialist Ethic*, University of Michigan Press, Ann Arbor, 1960.
Jeanson, F., *Le Problème moral et la Pensée de Sartre*, Myrthe, 1947. *Sartre par lui-même*, Le Seuil, 1954.
Murdoch, I., *Sartre: Romantic Rationalist*, Bowes & Bowes, Cambridge, 1953; Yale University Press, 1953.
Thody, P., *Jean-Paul Sartre: A Literary and Political Study*, Hamish Hamilton, London, 1960; Macmillan, New York, 1961.

Marcel, Gabriel, *Le Déclin de la Sagesse*, Plon, 1954. *La Dignité Humaine*, Vitta, 1955 (*The Existential Background of Human Dignity*, Harvard Univ. Press, 1965). *Etre et Avoir*, Aubier, 1933 (Peter Smith, Gloucester, Mass.). *Fragments Philosophiques*, Nauwelaerts, 1964 (Univ. of Notre Dame Press, Notre Dame, Ind., 1965). *L'Homme Problématique*, Aubier, 1955. *Les Hommes contre l'Humain*, La Colombe, 1951 (*Man Against Mass Society*, Regnery, Chicago, 1962). *Homo Viator*, Aubier, 1945 (Harper & Row, New York). *Journal Métaphysique*, Gallimard, 1927 (Regnery, 1967). *La Métaphysique de Royce*, Aubier, 1945. *Le*

Mystère de l'Etre, Aubier, 1951 (Regnery, 1960). *Paix sur la Terre*, Aubier, 1965. *Position et Approches du Mystère ontologique*, Nauwelaerts & Vrin, 1945. *Présence et Immortalité*, Flammarion, 1959 (Duquesne Univ. Press, Pittsburgh, Pa., 1967). *Du Refus à l'Invocation*, Gallimard, 1940.

Davy, M.-M., *Un Philosophe Itinérant—Gabriel Marcel*, Flammarion.
Parain-Vial, J., *Gabriel Marcel*, Seghers, 1966.

Lavelle, Louis, *La Conscience de Soi*, Grasset, 1933. *La Dialectique de l'Eternel Présent: De l'Etre*, Alcan, 1927; *De l'Acte*, Aubier, 1937; *Du Temps et de l'Eternité*, Aubier, 1945; *La Présence totale*, Aubier, 1934. *L'Erreur de Narcisse*, Grasset, 1939 (*Dilemma of Narcissus*, Allen & Unwin, London; Humanities Press, New York, 1973). *Le Mal et la Souffrance*, Plon, 1940. *La Parole et l'Ecriture*, L'Artisan du Livre, 1942.
Maritain, Jacques, *Art and Poetry*, Kennikat, Port Washington, York, 1969. *Art et Scolastique*, Desclée de Brouwer, 1920 (Sheed & Ward, London; Books for Libraries, Freeport, New York, 1962). *Creative Intuition in Art and Poetry*, Princeton Univ. Press, 1953. *Distinguer pour Unir, ou les Degrés du Savoir*, Desclée de Brouwer, 1932. *Eléments de Philosophie*, Tequi, Paris, 2 vols, 1920–23 (*An Introduction to Philosophy*, Sheed & Ward, London, 1930; New York, 1956). *Freedom and the Modern World*, Sheed & Ward, London; Gordian Press, New York, 1971. *On the Philosophy of History*, Bles, London, 1959; Scribner, New York, 1959. *Le Paysan de la Garonne*, Desclée de Brouwer, 1966 (Chapman, London, 1968; Holt, Rinehart & Winston, New York, 1968). *The Range of Reason*, Scribner, New York, 1952; Bles, London, 1953. *Redeeming the Time*, Bles, London, 1943; Hillary, New York, 1943. *The Rights of Man and Natural Law*, Bles, London, 1963; Gordian Press, New York, 1972. *St Thomas Aquinas*, Sheed & Ward, London and New York, 1931. *Science and Wisdom*, Bles, London, 1940; Scribner, New York, 1940. *The Scope of Demythologizing*, SCA. *Twilight of Civilization*, Bles, London; Sheed & Ward, New York, 1943.

Camus, Albert, *L'Exil et le Royaume*, Gallimard, 1957 (Hamish Hamilton, London; Knopf, New York, 1958). *L'Homme révolté*, Gallimard, 1951 (*The Rebel*, Hamish Hamilton, 1953; Knopf, 1954). *Le Mythe de Sisyphe*, Gallimard, 1942 (Hamish Hamilton; Knopf, 1955). *La Peste*, Gallimard, 1947 (Hamish Hamilton, London, 1948; Knopf, New York, 1948).

Cruikshank, J., *Albert Camus and the Literature of Revolt*, Oxford Univ. Press, 1959.

King, A., *Camus*, Oliver & Boyd, Edinburgh and London, 1964.

Thody, P., *Albert Camus*, London, 1957.

Weil, Simone, *Attente de Dieu*, Colombe, 1950 (Fontana, London, 1959; Harper & Row, New York, 1973). *Cahiers*, Plon, vol. I, 1951; II, 1953; III, 1956 (*First and Last Notebooks*, Oxford Univ. Press, London and New York, 1970). *La Condition ouvrière*, Gallimard, 1951. *La Connaissance Surnaturelle*, Gallimard, 1950. *Ecrits historiques et politiques*, Gallimard, 1960. *L'Enracinement*, Gallimard, 1949. *Intuitions pré-chrétiennes*, Colombe, 1951. *Leçon de Philosophie*, Plon, 1959. *Lettre à une Religieuse*, Gallimard, 1951. *Pensées sans ordre concernant l'amour de Dieu*, Gallimard, 1962. *La Pesanteur et la Grâce*, Plon, 1944 (Routledge & Kegan Paul, London, 1952). *Les Sources grecques*, Gallimard, 1953. *Sur la Science*, Gallimard, 1966 (*On Science, Necessity and the Love of God*, Oxford Univ. Press, London and New York, 1968).

Davy, M.-M., *Simone Weil*, PUF, 1967.

Pétrement, S., *Simone Weil*, Fayard, 1973.

Teilhard de Chardin, Pierre, *L'Activation de l'Energie*, Le Seuil, 1963 (Collins, London, 1970; Harcourt Brace, New York, 1971). *L'Apparition de l'Homme*, Le Seuil, 1956 (Collins, 1965). *L'Avenir de l'homme*, Le Seuil, 1959 (Collins, 1964; Harper & Row, New York, 1969). *Ecrits du temps de la guerre*, Grasset, 1965 (Collins, 1968). *L'Energie humaine*, Le Seuil, 1962 (Collins, 1969; Harcourt Brace, 1971). *La Messe sur le Monde*, Le Seuil, 1965 (*Hymn of the Universe*, Collins; Harper & Row, 1965). *Le Milieu Divin*, Le Seuil, 1957 (Collins, 1960; Harper). *Le Phénomène Humain*, Le Seuil, 1955 (Collins, 1955; Harper). *La Place de l'Homme dans la Nature*, Le Seuil, 1963 (Collins, 1966; Harper & Row, 1973). *Science et Christ*, Le Seuil, 1957 (Collins, 1968). *La Vision du passé*, Le Seuil, 1957 (Collins, 1966; Harper & Row, 1967).

Cuénot, C., *P. Teilhard de Chardin: les grandes étapes de son évolution*, Plon, 1958.

De Lubac, P., *La Pensée religieuse du Père Teilhard de Chardin*, Aubier, 1961.

Bachelard, Gaston, *La Dialectique de la Durée*, PUF, 1936. *L'Eau et les Rêves*, Corti, 1942. *Essai sur la Connaissance approchée*, Vrin, 1928. *La Formation de l'Esprit scientifique*, Vrin, 1938. *L'Intuition de l'Instant*, Stock, 1935. *Le Matérialisme rationnel*, PUF, 1963. *La Philosophie du Non*, PUF, 1966 (Grossman, New York, 1968). *La Poétique de l'Espace*, PUF, 1957 (Grossman, 1964). *La Poétique de la Rêverie*, Corti, 1961 (Grossman, 1969). *La Psychanalyse du feu*, Gallimard, 1938 (Routledge & Kegan Paul, London; Beacon Press, Boston, Mass., 1964). *Le Rationalisme appliqué*, PUF, 1966. *La Terre et les Rêveries du Repos*, Corti, 1948. *La Terre et les Rêveries de la Volonté*, Corti, 1948.

Lévi-Strauss, Claude, *Anthropologie Structurale*, Plon, 1958 (Basic Books, New York, 1963; Allen Lane, London, 1968). *Anthropologie Structurale II*, Plon, 1973. *Le Cru et le Cuit*, Plon, 1964 (Harper & Row, New York, 1969). *Du Miel aux Cendres*, Plon, 1966 (Cape, London; Harper & Row, 1973). *L'Origine des manières de table*, Plon, 1968. *La Pensée Sauvage*, Plon, 1962 (Weidenfeld & Nicolson, London; Univ. of Chicago Press, 1966). *Les Structures élémentaires de la Parenté*, PUF, 1949 (Beacon Press, Boston, Mass., 1969; Tavistock, London, 1970). *Le Totémisme aujourd'hui*, PUF, 1962 (Beacon Press, 1963; Penguin, London, 1969). *Tristes Tropiques*, Plon, 1955 (Atheneum, 1964).

Auzias, J.-M., *Clefs pour le Structuralisme*, Seghers, 1967.
Leach, E., *Lévi-Strauss*, Collins, London, 1970.

Foucault, Michel, *Maladie mentale et Personnalité*, PUF, 1970. *Les Mots et les Choses*, Gallimard, 1966. *Archaeology and Knowledge*, Tavistock, London; Pantheon, New York, 1972. *Madness and Civilisation*, Pantheon, 1965; Tavistock, 1971.

Althusser, Louis, *Lénine et la Philosophie*, Maspero, 1972 (New Left Books, London, 1971; Monthly Review Press, New York, 1972). *Lire 'Le Capital'*, Maspero, 1965 (Allen Lane, London, 1970; Pantheon, New York). *Pour Marx*, Maspero, 1966. *Réponse à John Lewis*, Maspero, 1973.

Lacan, Jacques, *Ecrits*, Le Seuil, 1966.
Derrida, Jacques, *La Voix et le Phénomène*, PUF, 1967. *L'Ecriture et la Différence*, Le Seuil, 1969.

INDEX

Italicised page references indicate major treatment

Sartre, Jean-Paul, *(cont.)*
anguish of choice, 103–4; bad faith, 104, 109, 124; on Baudelaire, 104–5, 124; Being denied by, 100–1; on Camus, 134, 135; conscious deliberation is fake, 102; consciousness, 100, 102–3, 105–6, 108, 110, 111–12, 158; *Critique de la Raison Dialectique*, 108, 112–13; *Le Diable et le Bon Dieu*, 114–15; dramatic works, 114–16; essence, notion of, 89, 95, 100, 127; *L'Etre et le Néant*, 93, 94, 96, 97, 99, 100, 101–4, 105, 108, 112, 113, 123; existence precedes essence for man, 94, 95; *L'Existentialisme est un Humanisme*, 94–5, 98, 99; freedom and choice, 29, 93, 94–5, 96–8, 100, 101–4, 109, 110, 123; *Huis Clos*, 108, 115, 116; human nature repudiated by, 95, 96, 103; human responsibility, 96, 103–4, 128; *L'Imaginaire*, 106–8; *in-se* and *per-se* (in-itself and for-itself), 69, 70, 80, 93, 103, 105–8, 121, 158; love, notion of, 110–11; *Les Mains Sales*, 115; man aspires to be God, 52, 61, 95, 96, 136; man condemned to be free, 86, 101–2, 112, 123; Marxism and, 73, 108, 112–13; Merleau-Ponty and, 68–9, 80; *Les Mots*, 116; *Les Mouches*, 115, 123; nausea, 104, 108, 135; *La Nausée*, 101, 116; nothingness, 60, 80, 83, 93, 96, 98–100, 103, 105, 106, 107, 109, 111–12, 158; possession, 111; the self and the other, 65, 69, 93, 96, 103–4, 108–12, 124, 164; *Les Séquestrés de l'Altona*, 115–16; shame in the face of the other, 108–10, 111; *Situations*, 68, 116
Saussure, Ferdinand, 165
Schelling, F. W. J. 22
Schopenhauer, Arthur, 22, 156, 185
science, scientific thought, 17, 43, 189; Bachelard's epistemology of, 155, 156; Bergson's views and method, 23, 26, 43, 57, 78, 148; dissolution of man as final goal of (Lévi-Strauss), 169, 179; Greek, 12–13; Merleau-Ponty's views, 72, 77–8; 19th-century belief in supreme value of, 22; structuralist approach to, 179, 180–1, 183–4; Teilhard's reconcilia-

tion of religion and, 143, 145, 147, 148–9
self-knowledge, 10; Bachelard's moments of perfect, 157–8; evolution in life towards, 34–5; Greek consciousness of necessity acquired through, 12
semiology, 166
Shakespeare, William, 38, 175, 179
Socrates, 11, 12, 47, 88, 122, 142, 185, 190; Christ and, 44–5
Song of Songs, 48
soul: as mediating link between Time and the Divine, 12; Merleau-Ponty's concept of body and, 82–3; mysticism and, 50; primitive society's notion of, 47–8; Simone Weil's detachment of body from, 142
space: discontinuity of movement in, 43; duration and, 27, 54; Kant's pure intuition of time and, 27, 43, 58; structuralist view of, 163; time and, 40–1
Spencer, Herbert: evolutionism, 16, 23, 34, 35; intelligence, 35; mechanistic notion of time, 23–4
Spinoza, Baruch, 13, 58, 96, 140, 162, 182
spirit: Bergson's separation of matter from, 31, 35, 40, 148; Lavelle's notion of, 126–7; Teilhard's spiritualisation of matter, 147, 148
Spurgeon, Caroline, 159
Stael, Mme de, 155
Starobinski, 155
stream of consciousness, 20
structuralism, 155, *161–87*; Althusser, 178–83; Barthes, 176; Foucault, 177–8; Lacan, 176–7; language and literature, 170–7, 178, 183, 184–6; Lévi-Strauss, 162, 163–70; scientific positivism of, 183–4
subconscious, 20, 42, 159, 161; Lévi-Strauss's concern with, 165, 167, 177; pre-reflective world distinct from, 70; structuralist view of, 162, 175, 176–7; Surrealist and Dadaist liberation of, 57
subjectivity, 70; as basis of existentialism, 92, 118–19; Bachelard's notion of, 159; and Merleau-Ponty, 70, 72–3; objectivity v., 62–3; of language, 171; transcendental, 65, 157